30 Lessons on GRAMMAR

Michael A. Putlack

DARAKWON

30

Lessons on

GRAMMAR

Author Michael A. Putlack
Publisher Chung Kyudo
Editors Kwak Bitna, Cho Sangik
Designers Park Bohee, Lee Seunghyun
Illustrator Han Hyoseon
Photo Credit www.shutterstock.com

First Published August 2020
By Darakwon Inc.
Darakwon Bldg., 211, Munbal-ro, Paju-si, Gyeonggi-do 10881
Republic of Korea

Tel. 82-2-736-2031 (Ext. 553)

Price ₩15,000
ISBN 978-89-277-0984-8 13740
http://www.darakwon.co.kr

Main Book / Free MP3 Available Online
7 6 5 4 3 2 1   20 21 22 23 24

Introduction

One of the most common comments students make about learning English is, "Grammar is too hard." With that in mind, a team at Darakwon set out to create a grammar book that would make the study of English grammar much easier. The result of this effort is *30 Lessons on Grammar*.

As the title indicates, this book contains thirty individual lessons covering various aspects of English grammar. The grammar lessons in each unit are explained in a simple and direct manner. Then, there are example sentences illustrating exactly how to use the grammar readers have just learned. Finally, there are a number of exercises for readers to practice the material covered in the units so that they can have a complete understanding of it.

Upon reaching the end of the book, readers should have an outstanding understanding of many aspects of English grammar. They should be able to use this knowledge to improve their reading, listening, speaking, and writing skills in English.

This book is designed so that readers can use it in a variety of ways. They may opt to use this book as they study by themselves. They may also use this book in a classroom environment as they study with other students. Readers may study the book unit by unit starting from the beginning. Or they may go over the material in the order in which they want to learn it. Whatever they choose to do, by focusing hard on the material, readers should be able to improve their knowledge of the English language.

I would like to thank my editor, Kwak Bitna, for her tireless efforts in working on this book. Without her, this book would not have been published.

I wish you the best of luck in your studies. May you find this book helpful.

Michael A. Putlack

Contents

Key Features

The lessons are taught in a manner that makes learning English grammar easy.

The exercises are fun for readers to complete, so studying with the book is entertaining.

Easy

Fun

Educational

Compact

The book is educational for readers as they will obtain a comprehensive understanding of English grammar by using it.

The lessons are compact, so readers do not get overwhelmed with material. Instead, they can study short, concise lessons that get right to the point.

An Overview

→ ### Unit Sentence
This sentence contains the grammar taught in the unit. It allows readers to understand what the grammar they are going to learn will be like prior to studying the unit.

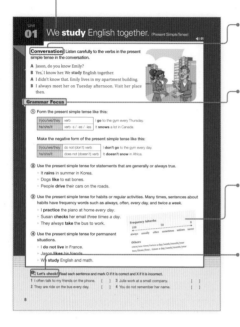

Conversation
The short conversation contains multiple uses of the grammar taught in the unit. This allows readers to learn how to use the grammar in practical situations.

Grammar Focus
This section provides comprehensive explanations of the grammar taught in the unit. There are also example sentences for readers to learn how to use the grammar properly.

Note
The note provides additional information related to the grammar in the unit.

Let's Check!
These four sentences allow readers to check their understanding of the material taught in the unit. Readers must determine if the sentences use correct or incorrect grammar.

Exercise I
This section contains two different exercises that allow readers to test their knowledge of the grammar taught in the unit. The exercises often differ from unit to unit, so readers can practice in a wide variety of ways.

Switch It Up!
This section provides a fun exercise that often requires readers to work and speak together with a partner or in a group.

Exercise II

This section contains one or two different exercises that are more challenging than the exercises in Exercise I.

Vocabulary

Definitions of difficult words and phrases in Exercise I and Exercise II are provided for readers.

Grammar Plus⁺

This section contains an additional grammar lesson that is connected to the information taught in Grammar Focus.

Grammar in Action

This section contains three short conversations. Readers must use the knowledge they learn in Grammar Plus⁺ to complete the conversations.

Chapter Overview

This graphic organizer briefly summarizes all of the information taught in the unit.

Exercise II

A Unscramble the words to complete the sentences.

1 Linda / meet / for lunch / Mark / at a restaurant / and

2 the cars / the red light / stop /at

3 I / at / lock / always / night / the door

4 on Saturdays / her bedroom / Irene / not / does / clean

5 a test / the teacher / gives / Friday / every

6 on / read / the Internet / the newspaper / they

7 we / house / in a big / live / do / not

8 cook / twice / I / with my husband / a week / dinner

lock *(v)* to fasten something with a key

B Correct the underlined parts in the paragraph.

Jonathan's Routine

Jonathan is a famous baker. He is hardworking and punctual. He ¹alway ²get up at three A.M. every night and ³is bake his products. Then, he ⁴have breakfast with his wife and ⁵is opens his bakery. His wife usually ⁶make his favorite pear marmalade for breakfast. Many customers ⁷comes to his bakery during the afternoon. At noon, he does not ⁸has lunch at his store. He leaves his son at the bakery and eats lunch at home. Then, he returns to the shop and chats with his favorite customers.

punctual *(adj)* at the right time and not late

product *(n)* something that is made and sold

marmalade *(n)* a food made from oranges, lemons, or grapefruit that is similar to jam

customer *(n)* someone who buys goods or services

10

Grammar Plus⁺

Use the present simple tense to talk about future events. These events are usually specific times or fixed plans.
▸ The game **starts** tomorrow at three o'clock.
▸ The train **leaves** the station in ten minutes.
▸ Mr. Reynolds **calls** his wife this evening.

Use the present simple tense to talk about future events with words such as *when, before,* and *after.*
▸ *When* it **snows,** we **will make** a snowman.
▸ I **will call** you *before* I **go** to the theater.
▸ *After* she **sees** the concert, she **will have** dinner.

Grammar in Action | Fill in the blanks with the words. Then, practice the dialogs with your partner.

1 A Is that Ms. Carter's plane?
   B No, it isn't. Her plane _____ in thirty minutes. (arrive)

2 A It rains a lot in spring here.
   B Yeah. When it _____, I will stay indoors. (rain)
   A Me, too. I don't go out in the rain.

3 A Before the movie _____, everyone will go to a coffee shop. (start)
   B I do not like coffee.
   A I didn't know that about you.

Chapter Overview

Review the information you learned in this unit.

generally or always true

permanent situations

Present Simple Tense

habits or regular activities

future events

We **study** English together. (Present Simple Tense)

Conversation | Listen carefully to the verbs in the present simple tense in the conversation.

A Jason, do you know Emily?

B Yes, I know her. We **study** English together.

A I didn't know that. Emily lives in my apartment building.

B I always meet her on Tuesday afternoon. Visit her place then.

Grammar Focus

① Form the present simple tense like this:

I/you/we/they	verb	I **go** to the gym every Thursday.
he/she/it	verb -s / -es / -ies	It **snows** a lot in Canada.

Make the negative form of the present simple tense like this:

I/you/we/they	do not (don't) verb	I **don't go** to the gym every day.
he/she/it	does not (doesn't) verb	It **doesn't snow** in Africa.

② Use the present simple tense for statements that are generally or always true.

  ▹ It **rains** in summer in Korea.

  ▹ Dogs **like** to eat bones.

  ▹ People **drive** their cars on the roads.

③ Use the present simple tense for habits or regular activities. Many times, sentences about habits have frequency words such as *always, often, every day,* and *twice a week.*

  ▹ I **practice** the piano at home *every day*.

  ▹ Susan **checks** her email *three times a day*.

  ▹ They *always* **take** the bus to work.

④ Use the present simple tense for permanent situations.

  ▹ I **do not live** in France.

  ▹ Jason **likes** his friends.

  ▹ We **study** English and math.

Frequency Adverbs

100   50   0

always   usually   often   sometimes   seldom   never

Others

once/one time/twice a day/week/month/year

two/three/four... times a day/week/month/year

Let's check! Read each sentence and mark O if it is correct and X if it is incorrect.

1 I often talk to my friends on the phone.   [   ]   **3** Julie work at a small company.   [   ]

2 They are ride on the bus every day.   [   ]   **4** You do not remember her name.   [   ]

Exercise 1

A Complete the sentences in the present simple tense with the words in parentheses.

1 I _____ soccer every day. (not play)

2 Christine _____ to the mountains with her family. (travel)

3 Dave and Jay _____ history at their university. (learn)

4 It _____ cold in Singapore during winter. (not get)

5 We often _____ cookies on the weekend. (bake)

6 He _____ the Internet in his free time. (surf)

7 People _____ books at the bookstore in the shopping center. (buy)

during *(prep)* throughout a certain time

weekend *(n)* Saturday and Sunday

B Complete the sentences with the words in the box. You may need to change the forms of the words.

exercise	dance	eat	write	begin	watch	go

1 Sue _____ with her friends at the concert.

2 The workday _____ at nine in the morning every day.

3 People _____ at a gym for their health.

4 They _____ an action movie at the theater.

5 Rick does not _____ letters to his friends.

6 Sara _____ to the swimming pool after school.

7 Many people _____ bacon and eggs for breakfast.

workday *(n)* the time during a day a person works

health *(n)* the condition of the body and the mind

theater *(n)* a place people go to watch movies or plays

Switch It Up!

Look at the list of activities. Then, tell your partner how often you do these activities.

1 get up early

2 meet my friends

3 clean my room

4 arrive late at work/school

5 take a shower

6 use social media

7 cook dinner

8 forget something

9 drive a car

10 call my parents

11 go shopping

12 listen to music

I always get up early. But I never drive a car. I cook dinner every day...

Exercise II

A Unscramble the words to complete the sentences.

1 Linda / meet / for lunch / Mark / at a restaurant / and

_____

2 the cars / the red light / stop /at

_____

3 I / at / lock / always / night / the door

_____

lock *(v)* to fasten something with a key

4 on Saturdays / her bedroom / Irene / not / does / clean

_____

5 a test / the teacher / gives / Friday / every

_____

6 on / read / the Internet / the newspaper / they

_____

7 we / house / in a big / live / do / not

_____

8 cook / twice / I / with my husband / a week / dinner

_____

B Correct the underlined parts in the paragraph.

Jonathan's Routine

Jonathan is a famous baker. He is hardworking and punctual. He ¹alway ²get up at three A.M. every night and ³is bake his products. Then, he ⁴have breakfast with his wife and ⁵is opens his bakery. His wife usually ⁶make his favorite pear marmalade for breakfast. Many customers ⁷comes to his bakery during the afternoon. At noon, he does not ⁸has lunch at his store. He leaves his son at the bakery and eats lunch at home. Then, he returns to the shop and chats with his favorite customers.

punctual *(adj)* at the right time and not late

product *(n)* something that is made and sold

marmalade *(n)* a food made from oranges, lemons, or grapefruit that is similar to jam

customer *(n)* someone who buys goods or services

Grammar Plus⁺

Use the present simple tense to talk about future events. These events are usually specific times or fixed plans.

▸ The game **starts** tomorrow at three o'clock.

▸ The train **leaves** the station in ten minutes.

▸ Mr. Reynolds **calls** his wife this evening.

Use the present simple tense to talk about future events with words such as *when, before,* and *after.*

▸ *When* it **snows**, we **will make** a snowman.

▸ I **will call** you *before* I **go** to the theater.

▸ *After* she **sees** the concert, she **will have** dinner.

Grammar in Action | Fill in the blanks with the words. Then, practice the dialogs with your partner.

1 A Is that Ms. Carter's plane?

  B No, it isn't. Her plane _____ in thirty minutes. (arrive)

2 A It rains a lot in spring here.

  B Yeah. When it _____, I will stay indoors. (rain)

  A Me, too. I don't go out in the rain.

3 A Before the movie _____, everyone will go to a coffee shop. (start)

  B I do not like coffee.

  A I didn't know that about you.

Chapter Overview

Review the information you learned in this unit.

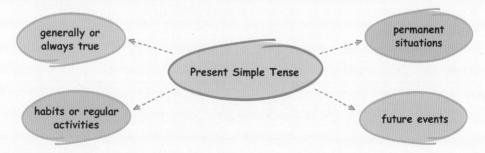

generally or always true

permanent situations

Present Simple Tense

habits or regular activities

future events

I'm checking my email on my phone.

(Present Continuous Tense)

◀)) 02

Conversation | Listen carefully to the verbs in the present continuous tense in the conversation.

A Hi, Mary. Are you busy now?

B Yes, I am. **I'm checking** my email on my phone.

A Do you want to have lunch now? Tom and I are going to a nearby restaurant.

B Sorry, but I can't. I have a meeting in a few minutes.

Grammar Focus

① Form the present continuous tense like this:

I	am + verb -ing	I **am studying** for a test now.
he/she/it	is + verb -ing	Janet **is talking** on the telephone.
we/you/they	are + verb -ing	We **are riding** on the bus.

Make the negative form of the present continuous tense like this:

I	am not + verb -ing	I **am not watching** TV right now.
he/she/it	is not (isn't) + verb -ing	He **is not cooking** dinner now.
we/you/they	are not (aren't) + verb -ing	They **are not staying** at a hotel.

② Use the present continuous tense for actions that are happening at the time a person is speaking. You should often use the words *now* or *right now* in these sentences.

▸ David **is writing** a report at his desk *now*.

▸ The boys **are playing** baseball together.

▸ Emily **is not surfing** the Internet *right now*.

> I **am** still **studying** at that academy.

You can also use the present continuous tense for actions that are not happening at the time a person is speaking.
Use the present continuous tense for ongoing actions and trends.

③ Use the present continuous tense for repeated sets of actions. You should use frequency words such as *always*, *usually*, or *frequently* in these sentences.

▸ Tim **is** *always* **arriving** late for school.

▸ I **am** *frequently* **forgetting** my possessions nowadays.

▸ They **are** *usually* **arguing** with each other.

🔎 **Let's check!** Read each sentence and mark O if it is correct and X if it is incorrect.

1 I am meet some friends right now. [ ] **3** We not are going on a picnic now. [ ]

2 You are asking some questions. [ ] **4** He is thinking about moving there. [ ]

Exercise 1

A Complete the sentences by using the words in parentheses in the present continuous tense.

1 Tim _____ the plants in his garden now. (water)

water *(v)* to give water to plants

2 Ms. Carter _____ her car to the city right now. (drive)

3 I _____ about a big problem. (think)

4 They _____ anything important now. (not do)

5 We _____ the offer by the other company. (consider)

consider *(v)* to think about

6 David and Tina _____ right now. (date)

7 Those boys _____ always _____ problems at school. (cause)

cause *(v)* to create or make

B Complete the sentences with the words in the box. Use the words in the present continuous tense.

get	order	look	buy	ask	ride	watch

1 I _____ for a new house in the city.

2 The customers _____ from the menu now.

3 Ms. Wilson _____ a new bike for her daughter.

4 Several people _____ the salesclerk questions.

several *(adj)* more than a couple but not many

5 Mr. Acuna _____ a job at a new company.

salesclerk *(n)* a person who sells things at a store

6 The fans _____ their favorite baseball team.

7 They _____ on the subway right now.

Switch It Up!

Tell your partner what each person is doing in the picture. Refer to the following key words if necessary: ride a bike, sit on a bench, swing, jog, roller-skate, talk on the phone, do yoga, play badminton, and jump rope.

Some people are spending time at the park...

Exercise II

A Correct the underlined parts.

1 That woman <u>are</u> working hard at her desk.

2 Sue and Mary are <u>swim</u> in the pool.

3 I am <u>playing not</u> on the soccer team this year.

4 Jason is always calling Tom and <u>ask</u> questions.

5 He <u>working</u> at a big company these days.   **these days** *(adv)* recently

6 We <u>am</u> not meeting anyone right now.

7 The patient <u>talking</u> to the doctor now.

B Rewrite the sentences in the present continuous tense.

1 He drinks coffee at a café.

2 Mr. Richards and his client talk about a business opportunity.   **client** *(n)* a customer
opportunity *(n)* a chance

3 I watch sports on television.

4 Susan still works at the same company.

5 The leaves change colors in fall.   **leaves** *(n)* the green parts of plants

6 Martin lives with his parents.

7 We eat a large pepperoni pizza for lunch.

Grammar Plus⁺

Use the present continuous tense to talk about future events. These actions and events are usually planned or prepared. Use future time expressions such as *tonight*, *tomorrow*, *in two days*, and *next week* to show you are referring to the future.

▸ My friend **is arriving** at the airport *tomorrow*.

▸ I **am taking** a Chinese class *next year*.

▸ We **are going** on a picnic *this weekend*.

Use the present continuous tense to talk about temporary events or situations.

▸ I usually watch TV now. But I **am doing** my homework instead.

▸ Lisa is a smart student. But she **is failing** her science class now.

▸ Mr. Jefferson is usually calm. But he **is yelling** at his employee now.

Grammar in Action | Fill in the blanks with the words. Then, practice the dialogs with your partner.

1 A Are you _____ up early tomorrow? (wake)

　B No, I'm not. Tomorrow is Saturday. I'm _____ late instead. (sleep)

2 A Karen, it's Monday morning. Why are you at home now?

　B I always go to work on Monday morning. But I _____ home today. I feel sick. (stay)

　A I'm sorry to hear that. I hope you get better soon.

3 A What are we eating for dinner tonight?

　B I am _____ chicken and rice. I _____ the chicken in the oven in ten minutes.

　　 (cook, put)

　A That's my favorite food. Thanks.

Chapter Overview

Review the information you learned in this unit.

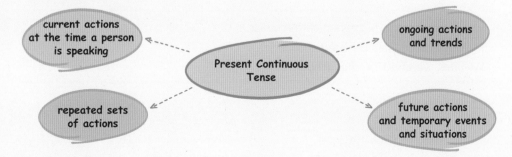

current actions at the time a person is speaking

ongoing actions and trends

Present Continuous Tense

repeated sets of actions

future actions and temporary events and situations

My wife and I **flew** to Australia in January.

(Past Simple Tense)

◀)) 03

Conversation | Listen carefully to the verbs in the past simple tense in the conversation.

A Jack, did you go on a trip last winter?

B Yes. My wife and I **flew** to Australia in January.

A I often visited Australia in the past. But I didn't go there last year.

Grammar Focus

① Form the past simple tense of regular verbs like this:

affirmative	verb + -d / -ed / -ied	The bus **arrived** on time.
		I **called** my friend on the phone.
		We **studied** in the library.
negative	did not + verb	Sue **did not watch** the movie.
		They **did not eat** dinner together.
		You **did not tell** me the truth.

*Add **-d** to verbs ending with a vowel and **-ed** to verbs ending with a consonant. Change *y* into *i* in verbs ending with *y* and add **-ed**.

The past simple tense forms of irregular verbs do not follow any patterns. You must memorize them.

| be – was/were   do – did   write – wrote   make – made   eat – ate   see – saw   win – won |
| come – came   go – went   drive – drove   read – read   ride – rode   teach – taught   have – had |

▶ Go to page 150 to see more past simple tense forms of irregular verbs.

② Use the past simple tense for actions that happened at a definite time in the past. You should use specific time expressions such as *last night*, *yesterday*, and *two days ago*.

  ▹ Tina **visited** her mother in the hospital *last night*.

  ▹ The soccer team **played** a game *three days ago*.

  ▹ I **did not talk** to my parents *yesterday*.

③ Use the past simple tense for actions that happened frequently in the past. You should use adverbs of frequency such as *always*, *usually*, *often*, *sometimes*, and *never*.

  ▹ We *always* **went** to the park near the forest.

  ▹ Mr. Davis *sometimes* **traveled** abroad.

  ▹ We *often* **watched** TV after school.

💬 **Let's check!** Read each sentence and mark O if it is correct and X if it is incorrect.

1 I did not ate anything this morning.　　　[　] 　**3** We joined the cycling club last week.　　　[　]

2 Ms. Hampton teached at a school.　　　[　] 　**4** She always sent her friends text messages.　[　]

Exercise 1

A Complete the sentences with the words in the box. Use the words in the past simple tense.

write	make	walk	drive	go	wrap	learn

1 We _____ in the forest for two hours yesterday.

2 Andy _____ the birthday present for his friend.

3 My father always _____ me to school in the morning.

4 She _____ a letter to her brother last Monday.

5 The students _____ math and science at school.

6 I _____ on a trip to India with my family.

7 Steve and Emily _____ dinner for some of their friends.

B Complete the sentences by using the words in parentheses in the past simple tense. Some sentences are negatives.

1 I was hungry, so I _____ a sandwich. (eat)

2 It was warm, so Sue _____ a coat. (wear)

3 She had trouble carrying the boxes. They _____ very heavy. (be)

4 The boys loved the movie. They _____ it two times. (watch)

5 I forgot my bank card. So I _____ the books. (buy)

6 Joe went to Fred's house. But Fred _____ home. (be)

carry *(v)* to move from one place to another

heavy *(adj)* weighing a lot

Switch It Up!

Using the keywords below, talk about the achievements of some historical figures. Choose the verbs from the box, change them into the past simple tense, and make sentences.

write	win	found	compose	~~paint~~	discover

Leonardo da Vinci, the *Mona Lisa*, in 1507   *Leonardo da Vinci painted the* Mona Lisa *in 1507.*

1 Christopher Columbus, America, in the 15th century   4 Shakespeare, *Hamlet*, in 1601

2 Beethoven, nine symphonies, throughout his life   5 Genghis Khan, the Mongol Empire

3 Albert Einstein, the Nobel Prize for Physics, in the early 20th century

Exercise 11

A Correct the underlined parts.

1 Mr. Conner <u>readed</u> a book last night.

2 The boys did <u>no</u> share their food with each other.

3 Angie <u>brushing</u> her teeth for two minutes yesterday morning.

4 I <u>eated</u> dinner with my friend last weekend.

5 We <u>ridden</u> in a car for about three hours this morning.

6 They <u>haved</u> a big house last year.

7 You often <u>did</u> swam in the pool a long time ago.

share *(v)* to use something together with others

brush one's teeth *(v)* to clean one's teeth with a toothbrush

about *(adv)* around; almost

B Look at Cathy's planner for October. Then, describe the activities she did during the last three weeks by making sentences.

Sunday	Monday	Tuesday	Wednesday	Thursday	Friday	Saturday
12 do online shopping	13	14	15 study Spanish with Suzy	16	17 attend her high school reunion	18
19	20 host a dinner party	21	22 go to the dentist	23	24	25 practice the piano
26 go to a rock festival	27	28 visit her parents	29	30 write a report at work	31	1 Today

She went to a rock festival last Sunday.

1 _____

2 _____

3 _____

4 _____

5 _____

Grammar Plus⁺

Use the past simple tense to talk about indefinite times in the past. Use past time expressions such as *in the past*, *a while ago*, *before*, and *a long time ago*.

▸ My parents **lived** in the countryside *a long time ago*.

▸ Joe **went** out with Susan *before*.

▸ I **knocked** on your door *a while ago*.

Use **did + verb** to emphasize a specific action.

▸ But I **did turn** off the TV last night.

▸ John did not travel to Hong Kong, but Stephanie **did go** there.

▸ The man **did drive** carefully. He did not drive too fast.

Grammar in Action | Fill in the blanks with the words. Then, practice the dialogs with your partner.

1 A You did not lock the door yesterday.

   B But I did _____ the door. Somebody else unlocked it. (lock)

2 A Did you travel to Paris last year?

   B No, I didn't. I _____ Paris a long time ago though. (visit)

   A Me, too. I _____ a great time there. (have)

3 A Did Stuart give that scarf to you?

   B Yes, he did. We _____ before. He _____ it for me then. (date, make)

   A Wow. I didn't know that about you.

Chapter Overview

Review the information you learned in this unit.

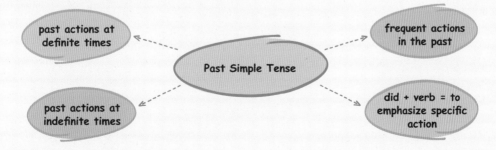

past actions at definite times

frequent actions in the past

Past Simple Tense

past actions at indefinite times

did + verb = to emphasize specific action

Have you **bought** your plane ticket yet?

(Present Perfect Tense vs. Past Perfect Tense)

◀)) 04

Conversation | Listen carefully to the verbs in the present perfect and past perfect tenses in the conversation.

A **Have** you **bought** your plane ticket yet?

B I had bought it, but then I canceled it.

A Why? Have you changed your mind about the trip?

B Yes, I have. I cannot go to South America this vacation.

Grammar Focus

① Form the present perfect tense like this:

affirmative	I/we/you/they	have + past participle	I **have seen** a giraffe before.
	he/she/it	has + past participle	The man **has finished** his work.
negative	I/we/you/they	have not + past participle	They **have not taken** the subway.
	he/she/it	has not + past participle	She **has not written** her report yet.

▶ Go to page 150 to see more past participle forms of irregular verbs.

Form the past perfect tense like this:

affirmative	had + past participle	You **had signed** the contract.
negative	had not + past participle	She **had not brought** any drinks.

② Use the present perfect tense in the following situations: 1) for an action that happened at an unidentified time in a person's life, 2) for an action or condition that started in the past and continues to the present time, and 3) for a repeated action sometime between the past and now.

  ▶ Alice **has met** the president *before*.

  ▶ I **have attended** this school *for six months*.

  ▶ He **has called** me *three times* today.

③ Use the past perfect tense to show that one action happened before another.

  ▶ I **had cooked** dinner before everyone *ate* it.

  ▶ Janet *was* sleepy because she **had stayed** up late.

  ▶ After they **had taken** a break, they *returned* to their office.

  *It is fine to use the past simple tense and not the past perfect tense with conjunctions such as *before* and *after*.
  I **cooked** dinner *before* everyone ate it.

💬 **Let's check!** Read each sentence and mark O if it is correct and X if it is incorrect.

1 Clara has met the president before. [   ]   **3** Because I had studied, I did well on the test. [   ]

2 They had watching the movie in the past. [   ]   **4** It have snowed here several times this year. [   ]

Exercise 1

A Correct the underlined parts.

1 They have <u>spend</u> some time in Japan.

2 Because you <u>has</u> apologized, I was not angry.

apologize *(v)* to say sorry

3 After Dave had <u>asks</u> a question, his teacher answered it.

4 The bell has not <u>stopping</u> ringing for ten minutes.

5 We <u>have</u> decided to watch the game, so we bought tickets.

decide *(v)* to choose to do something

6 Richard <u>have</u> sold his house already.

already *(adv)* by now

B Complete the sentences by using the words in parentheses in the present perfect or past perfect tense.

1 Jennifer _____ at the park several times this year. (jog)

2 Because it _____, Mark's family canceled their picnic. (rain)

cancel *(v)* to say a planned event will not happen

3 The stores _____ any sales in a long time. (not have)

4 Before she left her home, Alice _____ the windows. (close)

5 Kevin _____ with his boss about the problem. (speak)

6 Mr. Briggs _____ to my email yet. (not reply)

reply *(v)* to answer

7 Because he _____ the lottery, he bought a nice house. (win)

lottery *(n)* a gambling game in which people can win money

Switch It Up!

Find a partner and make questions and answers in the present perfect tense based on the phrases below.

travel to Thailand   3 cook dinner for a lot of people

1 meet a famous person   4 help a friend

2 do something dangerous   5 speak in front of many people

A *Have you ever traveled to Thailand?*

B *Yes, I have. / No, I haven't.*

Exercise II

A Complete the sentences with the words in the box. Use the words in the present perfect or past perfect tense.

try	grow	hear	pay	know	tell	sit

1 David _____ for the tickets before he picked them up.

2 Emily _____ Allen for more than ten years.

3 They _____ to fix the problem all morning.

4 Because I _____ him to be careful, he did not have an accident.

5 Mark _____ this song on the radio before.

6 Everyone _____ down before dinner started.

7 The farmer _____ corn since 2002.

pick up *(v)* to go somewhere to get something

fix *(v)* to repair

careful *(adj)* cautious

accident *(n)* something that happens by chance and often results in harm

farmer *(n)* a person who grows crops and raises animals

since *(prep)* between a past time and the present

B Unscramble the words to complete the sentences.

1 French / has / three years / she / studied / for

_____

2 I / I / number / did / because / had lost / her / not / call / her

_____

3 forgotten / past / you / have / your birthday / the / in

_____

4 the thief / the police / found / yet / have / not

_____

5 arrived / left / the office / when / he / she / already / had

_____

6 because / they / they / another country / go / their passports / had brought / to / could

_____

7 Mr. Wayne / Mr. Tanner / times / with / five / spoken / has

_____

arrive *(v)* to get to the place where one is going

passport *(n)* a document allowing a person to travel to other countries

Grammar Plus⁺

Use the present perfect tense for an action that was completed recently. Use the word *just* in these sentences.

▸ I **have** *just* **woken** up.

▸ She **has** *just* **talked** to her friend.

▸ The games **have** *just* **finished**.

Use the past perfect tense for an action that recently happened before another action. Use the word *just* in these sentences.

▸ I **had** *just* **hung** up the phone when it rang again.

▸ It **had** *just* **stopped** raining when it started again.

▸ She **had** *just* **stood** up when Mr. Anderson entered the room.

Grammar in Action | Fill in the blanks with the words. Then, practice the dialogs with your partner.

1 A Are you busy now? Let's go out somewhere.

  B I _____ lunch. Please wait a few minutes. (finish)

2 A Were you busy five minutes ago?

  B Yes. I _____ off the bus then. (get)

  A Oh, I see. I called you then, but you didn't answer the phone.

3 A Good news. Eric's plane _____. (land)

  B Great. I have just arrived at the airport. I will meet him soon.

Chapter Overview

Review the information you learned in this unit.

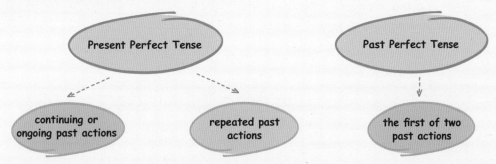

Present Perfect Tense

Past Perfect Tense

continuing or ongoing past actions

repeated past actions

the first of two past actions

I'm going to have dinner with some friends.

(Future Tense)

🔊 05

Conversation | Listen carefully to the verbs in the future tense in the conversation.

A Hi, Carol. What will you do tomorrow?

B I'm going to have dinner with some friends.

A I hope you have a great time.

B Will you join us?

Grammar Focus

① Form the future tense with **will** like this:

affirmative	will + verb	We **will work** hard tomorrow.
negative	will not + verb	Steve **will not take** a break tonight.

Form the future tense with **be going to** like this:

affirmative	am/is/are + going to + verb	I **am going to meet** some friends next week.
negative	am/is/are not + going to + verb	You **are not going to buy** anything soon.

② Use **will + verb** to predict future events, to express willingness to do something, to describe sudden decisions, and to give invitations in the form of questions.

▶ Terry **will have** a great time in China.

▶ I **will stay** late at the office with you tonight.

▶ Someone is at the door. I **will open** it now.

▶ **Will** you **have** lunch with me tomorrow?

You can use words such as *maybe, perhaps,* and *probably* to indicate that a future event might happen.

Maybe Jason **will show** up a bit late.
Perhaps it **will snow** a lot tomorrow.
I **will** *probably* **go** fishing this weekend.

③ Use **be going to** for future events that you decided to do in the past.

▶ "What **are** you **going to do** this summer?"

"I **am going to fly** to Hawaii this summer."

▶ Peter **is going to attend** college next year.

▶ The boys **are going to take** a test tomorrow.

💬 **Let's check!** Read each sentence and mark O if it is correct and X if it is incorrect.

1 Jason will apply for a job next week. [　] **3** I am going to call my friend in one hour. [　]

2 We are going to not have dinner soon. [　] **4** Mary will driving her car to work tomorrow. [　]

Exercise 1

A Complete the sentences with the words in the box and in parentheses.

be	turn	major	attend	buy	do	apply

1 They _____ a play this Thursday evening. (be going to)

2 I like that necklace. I _____ it right now. (will)

3 It _____ cold tomorrow morning. (will)

4 Emily _____ in economics at her university. (be going to)

5 David _____ for a job at that company. (be going to)

6 I can't hear the television. I _____ up the volume. (will)

7 Iris _____ probably _____ well at her performance tomorrow. (will)

play *(n)* a performance done on a stage

economics *(n)* the study of markets and how they work

probably *(adv)* maybe

performance *(n)* a type of entertainment done in front of an audience

B Complete the sentences by using the words in parentheses and either *will* or *be going to*.

1 _____ you _____ me some money today? (lend)

2 I have plane tickets already. I _____ to Europe this month. (fly)

3 Susan wants some groceries. She _____ to the supermarket now. (go)

4 Craig has other plans. He _____ a movie tonight. (not watch)

5 They have a test next week and need good grades. They _____ hard. (study)

6 It _____ probably _____ next January. (snow)

lend *(v)* to let someone borrow something

grocery *(n)* food and other items sold at a supermarket

grade *(n)* a score one gets in a class

Switch It Up!

Look at Mark's calendar for this week. Talk about his plans for the future by using *will* and *be going to*.

Sunday	Monday	Tuesday	Wednesday	Thursday	Friday	Saturday
1 Today	2 shop at an outlet store	3 have a business dinner	4 take the day off from work	5 go to a barbecue	6 relax at home	7 see a movie

Exercise 11

A Correct the underlined parts.

1 I <u>am</u> will read a book in my free time.

2 The post office is going to <u>delivering</u> packages next week.

3 Will you <u>driver</u> me to work tomorrow?

4 We are <u>going have</u> a picnic at the park on Saturday.

5 Are you <u>to going</u> finish your work soon?

6 Sam will <u>cooks</u> dinner for everyone now.

7 Helen <u>are</u> going to wear a blouse and jeans to the concert.

deliver *(v)* to take something to a person

package *(n)* a box with something inside it

B Match the sentences.

1 Will you tell me the answer? [ ]

2 Is Chris going to leave early? [ ]

3 Will the plane be late? [ ]

4 Am I going to get in trouble? [ ]

5 Are the stores going to open at nine? [ ]

6 Will Molly remember Steve? [ ]

7 Will you order fried chicken? [ ]

leave *(v)* to go away or depart

get in trouble *(v)* to encounter a problem

order *(v)* to direct that something be made or supplied

a. Yes, you are. You made a big mistake.
b. No, I won't. I will order a pizza.
c. No, he's not. He's going to stay until 10 P.M.
d. Yes, they are. They always do that.
e. No, I won't. I don't know it either.
f. Yes, she will. She has a great memory.
g. No, it won't. It will be on time.

until *(prep)* up to a certain time

either *(adv)* one or the other of two

memory *(n)* the ability to remember

on time *(adv)* not late

Grammar Plus⁺

Use **will** to make a prediction about the future based on an opinion.

▸ This movie **will be** so exciting.

▸ Dinner at John's house **will taste** delicious.

▸ We **will not have** fun at the party.

Use **be going to** to make a prediction about the future based on factual information.

▸ The score is 5 to 1. Our team **is going to lose** the game.

▸ The house is dark. Nobody **is going to answer** the doorbell.

▸ Irene is angry. She **is not going to let** you go home early.

Grammar in Action | Fill in the blanks with the words. Then, practice the dialogs with your partner.

1 A Look at the clouds. It _____ soon. (rain)

  B You're right. I will go home now.

2 A I _____ fun tonight. (have)

  B What are you going to do?

  A I'm going to watch a musical. It will be very impressive.

3 A Tomorrow _____ a bad day. (be)

  B I agree. We will take two exams tomorrow.

  A I'm going to study hard tonight. Then maybe I will do well on them.

Chapter Overview

Review the information you learned in this unit.

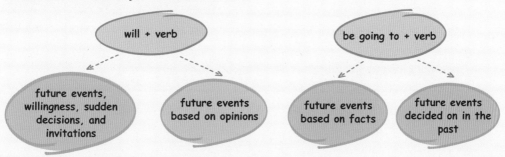

will + verb

- future events, willingness, sudden decisions, and invitations
- future events based on opinions

be going to + verb

- future events based on facts
- future events decided on in the past

May I **help** you with it?

(Modals I: Permission/Requests/Offers)

◀)) 06

Conversation | Listen carefully to the modal verbs asking for permission and making offers in the conversation.

A That bag looks really heavy. **May** I **help** you with it?

B Yes, please. Could you put it above my seat for me?

A Sure. I can do that for you.

B I really appreciate your assistance, sir.

Grammar Focus

① Use the following modal verbs to ask for and give permission, to make requests, and to make offers:

can		You **can use** my laptop for a while.
could	+ verb	**Could** you please **give** me some help?
may		**May** I **carry** that bag for you?

② Use **can** in informal situations.

  ▷ "**Can** I **go** out with my friends tonight?" "Yes, you can."

  ▷ "**Can** you **assist** me, please?" "No, I cannot."

  ▷ "I **can help** you solve that problem." "Thank you." / "That's okay."

  *When you give a short answer, use the same modal verb that is in the question.

③ Use **could** in more formal or polite situations. You can only use **could** to make requests and offers. You cannot use it to ask for or to give permission.

  ▷ "**Could** someone **lend** me some money?" "Sure." / "Sorry."

  ▷ "**Could** you please **turn** off the light?" "Okay." / "I'd rather not."

  ▷ "I **could give** you a ride to the bus station." "All right." / "Not right now."

④ Use **may** in more formal or polite situations. When asking questions with **may**, the subject must be *I* or *we*.

  ▷ "**May** I **sit** down here, please?" "Yes, you may." / "No, you may not."

  ▷ "**May** we **have** some more food, please?" "Sure. Here you are." / "Sorry. There's none left."

  ▷ "You **may stay** out late tonight." "Thanks." / "I appreciate it."

💬 **Let's check!** Read each sentence and mark O if it is correct and X if it is incorrect.

1 May you take a break right now?　　　[　]　**3** Could I answer the question, please?　　[　]

2 I can working late tonight at my job.　　[　]　**4** May I think for a few minutes?　　　　[　]

Exercise 1

A Complete the sentences by using the words in parentheses and the modal verbs *can, could,* and *may.*

1 I _____ the project for you. (finish / formal)

2 You _____ the work one day late. (complete / informal)

3 _____ I _____ your new bag tonight? (borrow / formal)

4 You _____ nicer to people from now on. (be / formal)

5 _____ you _____ me the location of the bank, please? (show / informal)

6 You _____ on this project with Tina. (work / formal)

complete *(v)* to finish

borrow *(v)* to use something from another person

location *(n)* the place where someone or something is

B Complete the sentences with the words in the box and the modal verbs *can, could,* and *may.*

borrow	meet	tell	wait	take	bake

1 You _____ her the answer to the question. (formal)

2 _____ you please _____ just a few more minutes? (formal)

3 _____ I _____ bicycle this afternoon? (informal)

4 You _____ a cake for the party. (informal)

5 _____ I _____ you on a tour of the city? (formal)

6 I _____ Mr. Burgess at the bus station. (informal)

Switch It Up!

Look at the different activities. With your partner, one student should ask for permission and make requests and offers, and the other student should respond.

Asking for Permission	Making Requests	Making Offers
Can I ~?	Could you ~?	May I ~?

1 borrow a laptop computer   4 cook dinner

2 pick someone up at the train station   5 help you with your project

3 turn down the music   6 make a suggestion

A *Can I borrow your laptop computer?*   **B** *Sorry. I'm using it now.*

Exercise II

A Correct the underlined parts.

1 May <u>you</u> watch television for a while?

2 I can <u>wrapping</u> all of those presents for the party.

3 Could you <u>don't</u> speak so loudly, please?

4 You may <u>visit not</u> your friends tomorrow.

5 May <u>talk I</u> with Mr. Wilson, please?

6 Could I <u>transfers</u> to another department?

for a while *(adv)* for a certain amount of time

wrap *(v)* to enclose something with a covering

loudly *(adv)* with a high volume

visit *(v)* to go to a place for a short amount of time

transfer *(v)* to move from one place to another

department *(n)* a section in a business

B Use the words to ask for permission and to make requests and offers. Add *can, could*, or *may* and choose other words from the box below to complete the sentences.

the solution	business card	some advice
the motor	your sweater	at 6:30 lunch

1 you / repair / please (informal)

2 I / have / your (formal)

3 you / explain / one more time / please (formal)

4 I / give / you (informal)

5 I / borrow / please (formal)

6 you / wake up / every day (formal)

7 I / buy / you / today (informal)

repair *(v)* to fix

explain *(v)* to make clear

Grammar Plus⁺

Use **can** to express an ability in the present tense. Use **could** to express an ability in the past tense.

▸ Ms. Waters **can speak** four foreign languages.

▸ I **can type** more than 100 words per minute.

▸ Thomas **could run** fast a few years ago.

Use **can**, **could**, and **may** to express a possibility. Use **can** to express a fact or a strong possibility. Use **could** and **may** to express a weak possibility.

▸ It **can be** difficult to live alone. Some people have problems.

▸ The report is complicated. It **could take** a long time to write.

▸ She **may arrive** on time. But she is usually late.

Grammar in Action | Fill in the blanks with the words. Then, practice the dialogs with your partner.

1 A My brother _____ soccer very well. (play)

  B So can I. I can also play volleyball and baseball.

2 A It can be hard to live in a foreign country.

  B You live in Russia, right? Can you speak Russian?

  A No, I cannot. I should study it though. I _____ it next year though. (learn)

3 A Your order _____ five days to arrive. It's the busy season. (take)

  B I need it faster though. Can you send it by express mail?

  A Yes, I can. With express mail, the order could arrive tomorrow.

Chapter Overview

Review the information you learned in this unit.

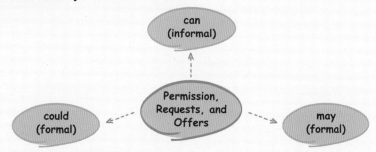

can
(informal)

Permission,
Requests, and
Offers

could
(formal)

may
(formal)

You **have to wake** up now.

(Modals II: Obligations/Responsibilities/Advice)

◀)) 07

Conversation | Listen carefully to the modal verbs indicating duties and responsibilities in the conversation.

A Dave, why are you still asleep? You **have to wake** up now.

B Yeah, I should get up. But I want to sleep more. I'm so tired.

A You shouldn't sleep anymore. It's already eight o'clock.

B Eight o'clock? Oh, no! I have to hurry to get to work.

Grammar Focus

① Use the following modal verbs to express obligations, responsibilities, and advice:

obligations, responsibilities	have/has to	+ verb	We **have to finish** this work by 6:00 P.M.
	must		I **must pay** back the money soon.
advice	should		You **should see** a doctor now.
	ought to		They **ought to study** harder in class.

② Use **have to** and **must** for obligations and responsibilities. With these modal verbs, a person is obligated to do something. It is that person's duty.

▸ You **have to mail** the letter today.

▸ Karen **has to pay** her rent tomorrow.

▸ We **must take** the bus at 6:30.

③ Use **should** and **ought to** to give advice and to make strong suggestions. With these modal verbs, a person is not required to do something. But it is a good idea to do the recommended action. **Should** is much more common than **ought to** in spoken English.

▸ I **should clean** my room right now.

▸ Robert **should apologize** to his friend.

▸ They **ought to go** out for lunch this afternoon.

💬 **Let's check!** Read each sentence and mark O if it is correct and X if it is incorrect.

1 I have to remember her phone number.　　[　]　**3** They ought to being quieter in the library.　[　]

2 You should to buy that leather jacket.　　[　]　**4** We must arrive at work before 9:00 A.M.　[　]

Exercise I

A Complete the sentences by using the words in parentheses and the modal verbs *have to, must, should,* and *ought to.*

1 You _____ carefully to your boss. (listen / responsibility)

    carefully *(adv)* with caution

2 He _____ a doctor as soon as possible. (see / advice)

3 I _____ my car this weekend. (wash / obligation)

4 Mr. Wright _____ his apartment today. (vacuum / strong suggestion)

    vacuum *(v)* to use an electronic cleaner

5 You _____ your sister some money. (lend / advice)

6 They _____ the grass at the park every week. (cut / responsibility)

    grass *(n)* small, thin plants that grow in yards

B Complete the sentences with the words in the box and the modal verbs *have to, must, should,* and *ought to.*

leave	wake up	take	buy	practice	eat

1 Greg _____ the piano for the concert every day. (advice)

2 You _____ these books for your class. (obligation)

3 We _____ early to get to the party on time. (suggestion)

4 Larry _____ early every morning of the week. (responsibility)

5 You are really hungry. You _____ dinner now. (suggestion)

6 Alice is flying to Poland tomorrow. She _____ her passport. (obligation)

Switch It Up!

Look at the signs in the box. Then, use *must* or *must not* to explain each sign.

1   2 BEWARE OF DOG 3 PLEASE KEEP OFF THE GRASS 4 NO PARKING TOW AWAY ZONE   5

I see a no-bicycling sign. You must...

Exercise II

A Correct the underlined parts.

1 George has to <u>getting</u> some rest tonight.

2 I must <u>to</u> stop waking up so late every morning.

3 You <u>ought go</u> on vacation in Australia.

4 Max should <u>asks</u> his friend for some advice.

5 We must <u>do</u> drive to the beach this weekend.

6 Wendy <u>have</u> to apply for a new job soon.

7 They ought to <u>will learn</u> to drive this winter.

B Unscramble the words to complete the sentences.

1 on time / you / finish / should / your chores

2 of the answers / I / all / to the questions / have to / memorize

3 he / tonight / must / his friend / at the theater / meet

4 the lights / somebody / off / turn / ought to

5 the girl / every morning / has to / her schedule / check

6 his house / the way / remember / to / you / must

7 the missing key / should / now / find / we

Grammar Plus⁺

Use **do not have to + verb** to say that something is not necessary to do.

▸ You **do not have to close** the door.   ▸ We **do not have to wash** the dishes.

Use **must not + verb** to order a person not to do something. It is required that a person not do a certain activity.

▸ You **must not talk** to strangers.   ▸ I **must not open** the door.

Use **should not + verb** and **ought not to + verb** to advise a person not to do something. The person could do the activity, but doing it is a bad idea. **Ought not to + verb** is not common in spoken English.

▸ You **should not drink** too much beer.   ▸ We **ought not to stay** out late tonight.

Grammar in Action | Fill in the blanks with the words. Then, practice the dialogs with your partner.

1 **A** I'm meeting my friends soon. We are going dancing.

  B You _____ dancing. You have a test tomorrow. (go / advice)

2 **A** Did you just take that candy bar? You _____ from stores. (steal / order)

  B But I'm really hungry. What should I do?

  A You should pay for that item right now.

3 **A** I'm tired. Do we have to go to the staff meeting?

  B We _____ it. But Mr. Wilson will be there. (attend / not necessary)

  A Oh, he's our boss. In that case, we should be there.

Chapter Overview

Review the information you learned in this unit.

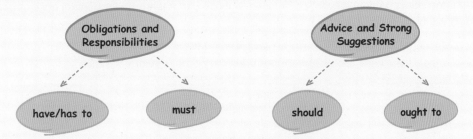

Obligations and Responsibilities — have/has to — must

Advice and Strong Suggestions — should — ought to

08 Can you repair a car? (Verbs of Ability)

🔊 08

Conversation | Listen carefully to the verbs of ability in the conversation.

A Tim, **can** you **repair** a car?

B I could do that in the past. But I can't fix any modern cars.

A Okay. I'll just call a mechanic then.

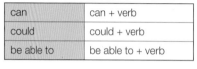

Grammar Focus

① Use the following verbs to talk about ability:

can	can + verb	I **can play** the piano.
could	could + verb	Tina **could sing** many songs.
be able to	be able to + verb	Craig **is able to speak** Russian.

Make the negative forms of the verbs like this:

can	cannot (can't) + verb	Larry **cannot drive** a car.
could	could not (couldn't) + verb	We **could not solve** the puzzle.
be able to	be + not + able to + verb	She **is not able to cook** Italian food.

② Use **can** to express an ability in the present tense. Use **could** to express an ability in the past tense.

  ▸ Ms. Waters **can speak** four foreign languages.
  ▸ Thomas **could run** fast a few years ago.

③ Use **be able to** to express an ability in any tense. It is also more formal than **can** and **could**.

  ▸ Mr. Stetson **is able to answer** that question.
  ▸ I **will be able to dance** well next year.
  ▸ They **were able to climb** the mountain.

④ Use **be able to** to express that you managed to do something. In addition, use **be able to** to describe a particular event or situation, but use **can** and **could** for general abilities or situations.

  ▸ The game is hard, but Stephen **is able to win** this time. (particular event)
  ▸ The game is hard, but Stephen **can win** every time. (general situation)

💬 **Let's check!** Read each sentence and mark O if it is correct and X if it is incorrect.

1 Harvey cannot understanding the teacher. [   ]   3 She could play soccer well in high school.   [   ]

2 I will be able fly an airplane soon.   [   ]   4 They can remember names very well.   [   ]

Exercise 1

A Complete the sentences with the words in parentheses and *can*, *could*, *cannot*, and *could not*.

1 The puzzle had too many pieces, so they _____ it. (solve)

   solve *(v)* to find the answer to a problem

2 Daryll enjoys cooking. He _____ all kinds of delicious dishes. (make)

3 I am sorry, but I _____ these instructions. (understand)

   instructions *(n)* orders or directions

4 When she was young, Jasmine _____ the violin very well. (play)

5 Mr. Peters _____ for everything since he has enough money. (pay)

6 She _____ David's phone number, so she did not call him. (remember)

B Complete the sentences with the words in the box and either *be able to* or *not be able to*. Write the words in the correct tense.

read	visit	win	complete	suggest	meet

1 Sorry, but we _____ your order right now.

   order *(n)* items that a person buys

2 We _____ Buckingham Palace if we go to London.

3 I _____ right now because I have other plans.

4 Ken _____ some ideas if you ask him.

5 Sally _____ books in Greek now very well because she studies hard.

6 Chester's team _____ the game against the other team last night.

   against *(prep)* in opposition to

Switch It Up!

Look at the list of activities. Talk with your partner about the activities that you can and cannot do.

1 speak in public
2 remember people's names
3 wait patiently for others
4 take care of a pet
5 work well with machines
6 jog for ten minutes
7 read a map
8 travel abroad alone
9 teach a friend something

I cannot speak in public...

Exercise II

A Correct the underlined parts.

1 John cannot <u>talks</u> about his problem with us.

2 I <u>will able</u> to assist you in two minutes.

    assist *(v)* to help

3 That <u>cannot</u> remain in the building after it closed.

    remain *(v)* to stay in a certain place

4 Brenda is not able <u>borrow</u> books from the library anymore.

5 The company <u>could</u> deliver the items by tomorrow morning.

6 The child was able to <u>attaching</u> the two blocks to each other.

    attach *(v)* to connect two or more things to one another

7 The bucket is too heavy, so he <u>can</u> carry it without any help.

    bucket *(n)* a pail used to hold things in

B Unscramble the words to complete the sentences.

1 install / the computer / you / can / on / the software

    install *(v)* to connect an electronic appliance

2 Mr. Arthur / this morning / could / the expert / not / with / consult

    expert *(n)* a person who knows a lot about a topic

    consult with *(v)* to seek advice from

3 a new club / able to / the students / are / at / establish / the school

    establish *(v)* to start a group, company, etc.

4 out / she / her friends / convince / to help / could / her

    convince *(v)* to change a person's mind about something

5 to learn / this summer / I / a new language / be able / will

    language *(n)* the entire group of words people use to communicate with

6 he / the show / able to / on television / was not / watch

7 in her room / cannot / her purse / Lisa / find / anywhere

    purse *(n)* a bag women use to carry money, cards, etc.

Grammar Plus⁺

Use short answers with only **can** or **could** to answer yes/no questions with **can** or **could**. You do not need to use the main verb in your answer.

▶ "**Can** you **ride** a bicycle?" "Yes, I **can**." / "No, I **cannot**."

▶ "**Can** Janet **write** the report?" "Yes, she **can**." / "No, she **cannot**."

▶ "**Could** Robert **play** the clarinet?" "Yes, he **could**." / "No, he **couldn't**."

Use short answers with only the **be** verb to answer yes/no questions with **be able to**. You do not need to use the main verb in your answer.

▶ "**Are** you **able to program** a computer?" "Yes, I **am**." / "No, I **am not**."

▶ "**Was** the man **able to find** his way home?" "Yes, he **was**." / "No, he **was not**."

▶ "**Will** Sara **be able to make** more money?" "Yes, she **will**." / "No, she **will not**."

Grammar in Action | Fill in the blanks with the correct words. Then, practice the dialogs with your partner.

1 A Sam, can you fix my computer?

   B Yes, I _____ . I have some free time now.

2 A Peter, are you able to work on Saturday?

   B No, I _____ . I have plans with my family.

   A Okay. Thanks for letting me know.

3 A I could dance well in the past. Could you?

   B Yes, I _____ . I did ballet as a child.

   A So did I.

Chapter Overview

Review the information you learned in this unit.

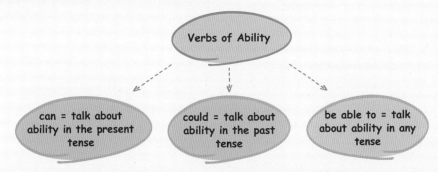

Verbs of Ability

can = talk about ability in the present tense

could = talk about ability in the past tense

be able to = talk about ability in any tense

It **was built** in 80 A.D. (Passive Voice)

Conversation | Listen carefully to the verbs in the passive voice in the conversation.

A Rome is so beautiful. When was it founded?

B It was founded more than 2,700 years ago. How do you like the Colosseum?

A I'm amazed by it. When was it built?

B It **was built** in 80 A.D. I'm surprised that it's so big.

Grammar Focus

① Form the passive voice in the present tense like this:

affirmative	am/is/are + past participle	History **is studied** by most students. I **am called** John by my friends.
negative	am/is/are + not + past participle	You **are not allowed** to enter the room. The man **is not noticed** by anyone.

Form the passive voice in the past tense like this:

affirmative	was/were + past participle	Jennifer **was remembered** by the people. They **were born** in Paris, France.
negative	was/were + not + past participle	She **was not given** a prize. We **were not pleased** with the results.

② Use the passive voice to show that the person or thing that experiences the action is more important than the person or thing doing the action. You can also use the passive voice to avoid showing who or what did the action.

▸ My house **was robbed**.

▸ The city **was founded** 250 years ago.

▸ The ground **is covered** with trash.

The thief robbed my house.

My house was robbed (by the thief).

③ Use the passive voice when speaking or writing in a formal manner.

▸ The air **is polluted** by factories.

▸ Gold **was found** in many places in Alaska.

▸ This day **is remembered** in history.

💬 **Let's check!** Read each sentence and mark O if it is correct and X if it is incorrect.

1 She was called on the phone by her friend. [   ] **3** The game was stopped due to the rain. [   ]

2 I am teached how to drive.   [   ] **4** We be given money for the trip.   [   ]

Exercise 1

A Complete the sentences by using the words in parentheses.

1 Sue _____ by the presents she got yesterday. (disappoint)

2 The room _____ by someone every night. (clean)

3 The children _____ cake and ice cream at the party last week. (give)

4 My house _____ more than 20 years ago. (build)

5 I _____ by the high price of the car. (surprise)

6 The movie _____ by a famous person last year. (direct)

7 The telephone _____ by Alexander Graham Bell. (invent)

direct *(v)* to guide the production of a performance

invent *(v)* to make something for the first time

B Complete the sentences with the words in the box. Use the words in the passive voice.

please	offer	consider	repair	teach	reward	train

1 Yesterday, the road _____ by a work crew.

2 Math and science _____ at every school.

3 I _____ a job to work at that company.

4 The workers _____ to use the software last week.

5 Mr. Jackson _____ a very intelligent man.

6 He _____ for catching the criminal by the police.

7 We _____ with the results of the test.

crew *(n)* a group of people working together for the same purpose

intelligent *(adj)* smart

criminal *(n)* a person who breaks the law

Switch It Up!

Read the questions and match them with the correct answers.

1 Who was the light bulb invented by?

2 When were the invitations mailed?

3 What was this house made with?

4 Who is taught to use the equipment?

5 What was said about the problem?

6 What animal is protected by the law?

7 When was he given the advice?

a. All employees are given instructions.

b. It was invented by Thomas Edison.

c. Dolphins are protected by the law.

d. It was built with bricks and concrete.

e. We were told it was fixed.

f. They were sent out last Friday.

g. He was advised a couple of days ago.

Exercise II

A Correct the underlined parts.

1 The game <u>are</u> watched by millions of people each year.

million *(n)* 1,000,000

2 The grade was <u>change</u> by the teacher.

3 The movie was <u>enjoying</u> by all of the fans.

4 Some houses <u>was</u> destroyed by the fire.

destroy *(v)* to turn something into useless pieces

5 The cake is <u>cooks</u> in an oven.

6 The trees were <u>cutting</u> down by the loggers.

logger *(n)* a person whose job is to cut down trees

7 His choice is <u>acceptance</u> by everyone else.

acceptance *(n)* the act of taking something offered

B Change the following sentences into ones using the passive voice.

1 The builders made the house.

2 Mr. Murphy explains the solution to the problem.

3 My mother cleans my bedroom.

4 The teacher criticizes the students.

criticize *(v)* to make negative comments about somebody or something

5 The librarian placed books on the shelves.

shelf *(n)* a thin piece of wood, metal, etc. that people place items on

6 The chef bakes pies in the oven.

7 The firefighters saved everyone from the fire.

save *(v)* to rescue from harm

Grammar Plus⁺

Use the infinitive form of the passive voice after modal verbs and other verbs that are usually followed by an infinitive.

▸ She had **to be told** about the problem.

▸ Steve wants **to be surprised** by the answer.

▸ I hope **to be pleased** with the painting.

Use gerunds after prepositions and with verbs that are usually followed by a gerund.

▸ Susan was pleased **about being invited** to the party.

▸ Mr. Jackson **likes being driven** to work in the morning.

▸ She **remembers being photographed** by the journalist.

Grammar in Action | Fill in the blanks with the words. Then, practice the dialogs with your partner.

1 A Why is Julie in Mr. Martin's office?

 B She needs _____ on her newest project. (instruct)

2 A Were you invited to dinner at the restaurant tonight?

 B Yes, I was. But I need _____ directions there. (give)

 A I was emailed them this morning. I'll send them to you later.

3 A You look really pleased about something.

 B I'm happy about _____ by my boss. (promote)

 A Congratulations. You will enjoy _____ more responsibilities. (give)

Chapter Overview

Review the information you learned in this unit.

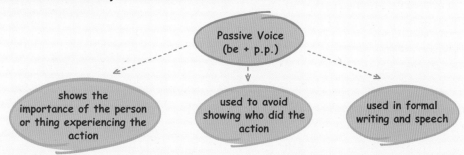

Passive Voice (be + p.p.)

shows the importance of the person or thing experiencing the action

used to avoid showing who did the action

used in formal writing and speech

I want **to learn** to ski. (To-Infinitives)

◀))10

Conversation | Listen carefully to the verbs in their to-infinitive forms in the conversation.

A I want **to learn** to ski.

B Me, too. But I don't have time to visit a ski resort.

A Oh, yeah? What are you planning to do this vacation?

B I haven't decided yet.

Grammar Focus

① Create the to-infinitive form of a verb by adding **to** in front of it:

to eat / to see / to learn / to go / to drive

② Use the to-infinitive to describe a purpose or to answer the question *why*. In these sentences, **to** means **in order to** or **so as to**.

▸ *"Why* did you call me?"

"I called **to ask** how you are doing."

▸ *"Why* did Lucy go to the library?"

"Lucy went to the library **to borrow** some books."

▸ *"Why* are they going out?"

"They are going out **to have** dinner."

③ Use the to-infinitive after verbs such as *like, love, hate, prefer, forget,* and *remember.* Many verbs which are followed by a to-infinitive refer to thinking, feeling, and speaking.

▸ Do not *forget* **to turn off** the computer tonight.

▸ Amanda *decided* **to take** a trip to India last week.

▸ He *prefers* **to stay** at home on the weekend.

④ Use the to-infinitive after adjectives to give reasons or opinions.

▸ I am *pleased* **to meet** you.

▸ The room is very noisy. It is *difficult* **to hear** you.

▸ I don't have any money now. It is *impossible* **to pay** for dinner.

💬 **Let's check!** Read each sentence and mark O if it is correct and X if it is incorrect.

1 Janet likes to playing sports.   [   ] **3** I wrote my friend to tell him some good news. [   ]

2 It is funny watch comedies at the theater. [   ] **4** Alice quit her job to move to another city.   [   ]

Exercise 1

A Complete the sentences with the words in the box in their to-infinitive forms.

solve	reserve	drive	lose	wear	eat

1 People learn _____ a car before getting a license.

2 It is difficult _____ puzzles with 1,000 pieces.

3 The weather is cold. We have _____ warm clothes.

4 Sue is hungry. She is ordering something _____ for lunch.

5 Did you remember _____ a hotel room?

6 Peter was disappointed _____ the game.

license *(n)* written permission from the government to do something

disappointed *(adj)* depressed or upset about something

B Correct the underlined parts.

1 I sometimes listen to music <u>for</u> relax.

2 It is wonderful to <u>trying</u> food in foreign countries.

3 Karen learns to <u>paints</u> at a private academy.

4 He wears a hat <u>protect</u> his head from the sun.

5 Robert is planning <u>taking</u> a trip to South America.

6 It is funny to <u>be heard</u> comedians tell jokes.

7 We looked at a map to <u>found</u> our way home.

foreign *(adj)* relating to another country

private *(adj)* belonging to a person

protect *(v)* to keep safe

joke *(n)* something said to make people laugh

Switch It Up!

Look at the picture of each person and that person's likes and dislikes. Then, tell your partner what each person loves and hates.

	John	Susan	Kevin	Helen
Likes	watch movies	drive cars	go scuba diving	jog at the park
Dislikes	visit coffee shops	wake up early	stay late at work	wait a long time

John loves to watch movies. But he hates to...

Exercise II

A Find the matching part for each incomplete sentence in the box and write the letter of the part in parentheses.

1 We contacted the bookstore [   ]

2 They were excited [   ]

3 The deliveryman came [   ]

4 Nancy and Joe like [   ]

5 We visited the supermarket [   ]

6 I called you on the phone [   ]

contact *(v)* to get in touch with

deliveryman *(n)* a person who brings things to other people

a. to buy some food for dinner.	d. to swim at the beach in summer.
b. to drop off a package for me.	e. to hear the good news from Tom.
c. to order some more books.	f. to ask about our homework.

drop off *(v)* to leave something for someone

B Use the words to make sentences with the to-infinitive. Add other words to complete the sentences.

I / like / play

→ *I like to play games with my friends.*

1 it / boring / stay

→

2 Lily / want / buy

→

3 Mr. Dawson / come / do

→

4 it / hard / argue

→

argue *(v)* to have a spoken disagreement with someone

5 I / call / ask

→

6 we / visit / see

→

Grammar Plus⁺

Use *too* or *enough* with an adjective in front of the to-infinitive. This lets people express why they feel a certain way.

▶ The soup is *too* hot **to eat** right now.

▶ I have *enough* money **to lend** you some.

▶ There are *too* many boxes **to put** in the truck.

▶ There is not *enough* space **to sit** on the ground.

Use the to-infinitive after wh-question words such as *who, what, when, where, how,* and *why*.

▶ My friend does not know *how* **to fly** an airplane.

▶ Everybody understands *what* **to do** tonight.

▶ Do you remember *when* **to arrive** at the train station?

Grammar in Action | Fill in the blanks with the words. Then, practice the dialogs with your partner.

1 A I want to ask you a few questions.

  B Sorry. I don't have _____ time _____ them. (answer)

2 A I am planning to visit Europe this vacation.

  B Who do you intend to go with?

  A I don't know _____ with yet. (travel)

3 A Let's have dinner at that restaurant.

  B Actually, that place is _____ expensive _____ at. (eat)

  A Okay. Then let's decide _____ next. (go)

Chapter Overview

Review the information you learned in this unit.

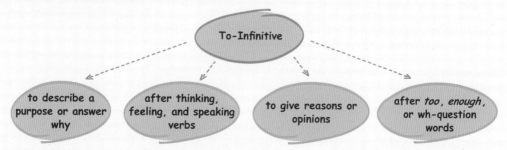

Watching movies is my hobby. (Gerunds)

◀)) 11

Conversation | Listen carefully to the gerunds in the conversation.

A Do you enjoy watching movies?

B **Watching** movies is my hobby. How about you?

A I enjoy reading books at my home.

Grammar Focus

① Gerunds are verbs that are used as nouns. Form gerunds by adding **-ing** to the base form of the verb.

running / playing / studying / going / coming / watching / listening

② Use gerunds as the subjects of sentences.

 ▶ **Driving** at night can be dangerous.

 ▶ **Studying** hard is important.

 ▶ **Eating** junk food makes people fat.

③ Use gerunds as the objects of sentences.

 ▶ I enjoy **watching** movies at night.

 ▶ Davie remembers **locking** the office door.

 ▶ Susan dislikes **playing** team sports.

*Sometimes two verbs may be used together. Some verbs must always be followed by a gerund. These include *admit, resist, delay, consider, discuss, enjoy, dislike, mention, avoid, mind, recommend, suggest, practice, involve,* and *miss.*

I *recommend* **waiting** for Bruce to call. (O)   I *recommend* **to wait** for Bruce to call. (X)
Jason *mentioned* **taking** a trip this weekend. (O)   Jason *mentioned* **to take** a trip this weekend. (X)
Carol *dislikes* **eating** at fast-food restaurants. (O) Carol *dislikes* **to eat** at fast-food restaurants. (X)

④ Use gerunds as complements of the *be* verb.

 ▶ His favorite hobby *is* **collecting** old coins.

 ▶ A difficult thing about my job *is* **staying** at work late.

 ▶ What Tom loves *is* **sleeping** late on weekends.

> **to-infinitives vs. gerunds**
>
> It is much more common to use gerunds as the subjects of sentences than to use to-infinitives as the subjects. Using to-infinitives is grammatically correct, but it can sound awkward, especially in spoken English.
>
> Exercising hard is good for your body. (O)
> To exercise hard is good for your body. (X)

💬 **Let's check!** Read each sentence and mark O if it is correct and X if it is incorrect.

1 Play soccer is lots of fun.   [   ]   3 My mistake was reserving tickets on the wrong day. [   ]

2 Joe forgot meeting Mr. Jacobs.   [   ]   4 The students love to watching movies at school.   [   ]

Exercise I

A Write the gerund forms of the verbs.

1 save: 5 play: 9 look:

2 keep: 6 lie: 10 take:

3 stop: 7 imagine: 11 quit

4 make: 8 run: 12 die:

lie *(v)* to say something false

B Unscramble the words to complete the sentences.

1 Simon / anything / saying / bad / to his friend / resisted

resist *(v)* to oppose doing something

2 free-time activity / his / reading / is / books / favorite

3 best skill / criminals / the policeman's / catching / is

catch *(v)* to capture

4 important / your friends / is / trusting

trust *(v)* to believe

5 ten minutes / answering / Rachel / the question / for / delayed

delay *(v)* to do something later than expected

6 texting / the driver's seat / one / from / major problem / is

major *(adj)* very big or important

7 recommends / healthy food / every day / Dr. White / eating

Switch It Up!

Underline the gerunds. Then, translate the sentences into your native language.

1 She loves talking to her friends on the phone.
2 Following the rules is important to do.
3 June's hobby is watching old movies.
4 I remember meeting my cousin last year.
5 Buying jewelry can be very expensive.
6 She tries exercising after work every evening.
7 What he remembers is locking the door.

Exercise II

A Correct the underlined parts.

1 The job involves <u>to work</u> late most evenings.

involve (v) to include

2 <u>Becomes</u> a doctor is her goal in life.

goal (n) an aim or objective

3 Roger considered <u>to ask</u> his boss for a raise.

raise (n) an increase in one's salary

4 The best reward is <u>get</u> time off from work.

reward (n) something given for doing a good act

5 The two men discussed <u>opened</u> a business together.

discuss (v) to talk about

6 <u>Please</u> her parents made her happy.

please (v) to make happy or satisfied

B Complete the crossword puzzle by using the words in the box. Change the words into gerunds.

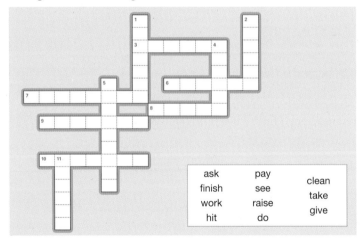

ask	pay	clean
finish	see	take
work	raise	give
hit	do	

raise (v) to take care of an animal

Across

3 Most people in big cities prefer _____ the bus.

6 The most important thing is _____ close attention.

7 One common task is _____ the house daily.

8 She thinks _____ homework is lots of fun.

9 David loves _____ at his company.

10 _____ animals on a farm can be difficult.

Down

1 He practiced _____ a baseball with his friends every day.

2 The woman reported _____ a man with a gun.

4 The owner dislikes _____ customers discounts.

5 _____ the work on time is our goal.

11 Edward's recommendation is _____ for assistance.

attention (n) notice

report (v) to state what one saw or heard

common (adj) usual

assistance (n) help

Grammar Plus⁺

Use gerunds after prepositions as well as after phrasal verbs that include prepositions.

- ▸ We are thinking *about* **signing** up for a conversation class.
- ▸ They avoided Mr. Jenkins *by* **walking** in the other direction.
- ▸ I look forward *to* **meeting** her in the future

Use gerunds as parts of compound nouns. Make sure that the gerunds have a noun meaning rather than a verb meaning.

- ▸ How about going to the **swimming** pool today?
- ▸ Chris is wearing his new **jogging** shoes now.
- ▸ Ed Sawyer's novel is a **bestselling** book.

Grammar in Action | Fill in the blanks with the words. Then, practice the dialogs with your partner.

1 A Where are you and Beth talking about _____ ? (go)
   B Hawaii is my goal, but she is considering flying to Cairo.

2 A Did you pay for everything by _____ your credit card? (use)
   B Yes. I didn't have enough cash on me.
   A You should avoid using your card too much.

3 A I should put these clothes in the washing machine.
   B Today is _____ day. I'll do some vacuuming. (clean)
   A Please clean the living room first since it's dirty.

Chapter Overview

Review the information you learned in this unit.

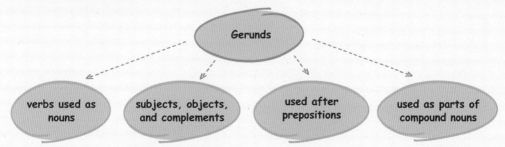

12 You should **stop coming** to work late.

(Verbs Taking To-Infinitives and Gerunds)

◀)) 12

Conversation | Listen carefully to the verbs that take to-infinitives and gerunds in the conversation.

A Jason, I regret to inform you that you didn't get the promotion.

B That's too bad. What did I do wrong?

A You should **stop coming** to work late.

B I always mean to do that, but it's hard to wake up in the morning.

Grammar Focus

① Use the **to-infinitive** after the following verbs: *want, agree, promise, learn, expect, decide, hope, agree,* and *need.*

▶ John **wants to go** on vacation.　　▶ We **learn to add** in math class.

Use **verb + -ing** after the following verbs: *finish, imagine, avoid, enjoy, consider, practice, deny, quit,* and *delay.*

▶ She **finished writing** her report.　　▶ The boy **avoids doing** his chores.

Use either the **to-infinitive** or **verb + -ing** after the following verbs: *start, begin, like, love, hate, continue,* and *bother.*

▶ He **started to watch** TV. / He **started watching** TV.

▶ Please **continue to talk**. / Please **continue talking**.

▶ *Go to page 152 to see more verbs which are followed by a gerund and a to-infinitive.*

② Use either the **to-infinitive** or **verb + ing** after the following verbs: *forget, remember, mean, stop, regret, go on,* and *try*. However, the verbs have different meanings.

refers to a past event	refers to a future event
I **forgot cooking** dinner for him last year.	I **forgot to complete** my report.
John **remembers meeting** Ms. Mercer.	John **remembers to lock** the door every day.
having to do something to get a result	intending to do something
This **means doing** work faster.	I **meant to take** the bus, but I missed it.
stopping an activity	stopping one activity to do another
Please **stop calling** me.	She **stopped to get** some rest.
being unhappy about a past activity	telling bad news to someone and being unhappy about it
Sylvia **regrets staying** up late.	Eric **regrets to inform** you that he is sick.

🗨 **Let's check!** Read each sentence and mark O if it is correct and X if it is incorrect.

1 Susan avoids to take the bus these days. [　]　　**3** You should stop saying bad words. 　 [　]

2 I regret to give you this bad news. 　 [　]　　**4** Keith meant losing weight. 　 [　]

Exercise 1

A Complete the sentences with the correct forms of the words in parentheses.

1 I promise _____ my best all of the time. (try)

2 Alice denied _____ the money from the box. (take)

3 Imagine _____ a big house in the countryside. (own)

4 They want _____ his birthday with a party. (celebrate)

5 You need to quit _____ so much noise. (make)

6 George hopes _____ the computer program this morning. (write)

7 Susan finished _____ her home one hour ago. (clean)

deny *(v)* to say that something is not true

countryside *(n)* a rural area that may have farms and no cities

noise *(n)* sound that is often loud and annoying

B Complete the sentences with the words in the box. Use the words in their correct forms.

rain	contact	arrive	spend	play	accept	hear

1 I enjoyed _____ time with my friends at dinner.

2 It suddenly began _____ about five minutes ago.

3 The boys learn _____ baseball after school every day.

4 Mary Ann forgot _____ her friend about the problem.

5 We hope _____ good news from Mr. Desmond soon.

6 The pilot expects _____ at his destination on time.

7 She will consider _____ the offer from the company.

suddenly *(adv)* happening without warning and by surprise

expect *(v)* to believe something will happen

destination *(n)* the place where one is going

offer *(n)* a proposal

Switch It Up!

Discuss the differences in the meanings of the pairs with your partner.

1 The woman **forgot to turn** off the light. / The woman **forgot turning** off the light.

2 The boy **meant to do** his homework. / The boy **meant doing** his homework.

3 She **stopped cleaning** her room. / She **stopped to clean** her room.

4 The man **regrets making** a big mistake. / The man **regrets to make** a big mistake.

5 She **remembered to go** grocery shopping. / She **remembered going** grocery shopping.

6 He **forgot meeting** the woman in the past. / He **forgot to meet** the woman in the past.

Exercise II

A Correct the underlined parts.

1 Mark often avoids <u>to have</u> arguments with other people.

2 I remembered to <u>telling</u> Mr. Nelson about the problem.

3 The employees want <u>receive</u> big bonuses this year.

4 Paul did not bother <u>write</u> down the message.

5 Ms. Dawson agrees <u>providing</u> consulting services for our firm.

6 Jason imagined <u>to win</u> the lottery and becoming a millionaire.

7 Please stop <u>talk</u> during meetings all the time.

B Unscramble the words to complete the sentences.

1 denied / the items / forgetting / Jeff / for / to pay

2 Roberta / wake up / early / to / in the morning / hates

3 your team / you / need / better / to manage

4 enjoys / during summer / at the beach / relaxing / Martha

5 we / a picnic / agreed / this Saturday / go on / to

6 after dinner / can / the book / reading / continue / you

7 stopped / a picture / of / landscape / the / beautiful / I / to draw

Grammar Plus⁺

Like can be followed by a gerund or a to-infinitive, and it has the same meaning. However, you should use **like doing** to describe an activity you enjoy. And you should use **like to do** to describe a habit.

▸ Chris **likes watching** television.   ▸ I **like to take** a walk in the morning.

▸ They **like learning** history.   ▸ Mr. Anderson **likes to check** his email after lunch.

Use **be used to doing** to indicate someone is familiar with an activity and **used to do** to indicate that someone did an activity in the past.

▸ I **am used to taking** the subway to work. (I still take the subway.)

▸ Clara **is used to cooking** dinner every night. (Clara still cooks dinner every night.)

▸ I **used to take** the subway to work. (I do not take the subway anymore.)

▸ Clara **used to cook** dinner every night. (Clara does not cook dinner every night anymore.)

Grammar in Action | Fill in the blanks with the correct words. Then, practice the dialogs with your partner.

1 A What do you like doing on weekends?

  B I like _____ movies. I also like _____ fishing every Sunday. (watch, go)

2 A How is your new job going?

  B It's a bit hard. I am used to _____ late. (wake up)

  A But now you have to get up early every day, right?

3 A Have you ever kept a diary?

  B I used to _____ in my diary every day. How about you? (write)

  A I haven't ever done that. But I would like _____ that. (do)

Chapter Overview

Review the information you learned in this unit.

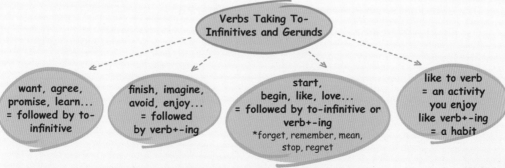

Verbs Taking To-Infinitives and Gerunds

- want, agree, promise, learn... = followed by to-infinitive
- finish, imagine, avoid, enjoy... = followed by verb+-ing
- start, begin, like, love... = followed by to-infinitive or verb+-ing *forget, remember, mean, stop, regret
- like to verb = an activity you enjoy like verb+-ing = a habit

◀)) 13

Conversation | Listen carefully to the participles in the conversation.

A You look **exhausted**, Stephanie. Are you okay?

B I'm fine. Don't worry. I was using the running machine at the gym.

A I'm surprised. I didn't know you exercised at a gym.

Grammar Focus

① Participles are verbs used as adjectives. Form the present participle by adding **-ing** to verbs. Form the past participle by adding **-ed** to regular verbs. The past participle forms of irregular verbs do not end in **-ed** and must be memorized.

② Use verbs in their present participle forms to show an ongoing action. They also show that the person, place, or thing they modify is doing the action.

▸ My friend is a very **caring** person.

▸ Look at the **running** man on the beach.

▸ We all enjoyed watching the **thrilling** movie.

③ Use verbs in their past participle forms to show that the person, place, or thing they modify had an action done to it. The past participle is typically used as a passive adjective.

▸ The **scared** boy is hiding under the bed.

▸ I want to repair this **broken** watch.

▸ We waited for the **frozen** fruit to thaw.

④ Be careful with words related to emotions and feelings. These include words such as *surprised* and *surprising*, *bored* and *boring*, and *thrilled* and *thrilling*. They have different meanings.

▸ I was **surprised** by the present.

▸ The **bored** girl is sitting in her room.

▸ We are **thrilled** to travel to Europe.

▸ The movie has a **surprising** ending.

▸ The **boring** boy has no friends.

▸ This book is so **thrilling**.

▸ *Go to page 153 to see more participle adjectives related to emotions and feelings.*

🗨 **Let's check!** Read each sentence and mark O if it is correct and X if it is incorrect.

1 Do you know the danced woman? [ ]

2 We watched some running dogs in the park. [ ]

3 He is playing an excited game. [ ]

4 I can see something burning. [ ]

Exercise 1

A Read the sentences and circle the participles. Then, underline the words modified by the participles.

1 That man painting is my good friend.

2 Firefighters hurried to the burning house.

burning *(adj)* being on fire

3 Sam put the trapped animal in a cage.

4 The disappointed girl got a poor grade.

5 I heard the telephone ringing.

6 Wilma likes to read printed books instead of e-books.

instead of *(prep)* as a substitute for

7 The eating dog is very hungry.

B Choose the correct words.

1 The (shining / shined) sun is very bright today.

2 (Blooming / Bloomed) flowers always smell nice.

bloom *(v)* to produce flowers

3 The (ringing / ranged) telephone belongs to Ms. Duncan.

belong to *(v)* to be owned by

4 No visitors can enter the (restricting / restricted) area.

restrict *(v)* to keep within a limit

5 Most people enjoy watching (marching / marched) bands.

march *(v)* to walk with regular steps

6 Julie often eats (precooking / precooked) meals for dinner.

7 People feel (annoying / annoyed) by the loud noise.

Switch It Up!

Look at each picture. Then, use the words to make a sentence with a participle to explain each picture.

the man, tire

the movie, terrify

the woman, surprise

the students, bore

the rollercoaster, thrill

the book, interest

The man looks tired. The movie is...

Exercise 11

A Complete the sentences by choosing the words from the box.

> sleeping / slept   growing / grown   flying / flown   losing / lost
> breaking / broken   smiling / smiled   processing / processed

process *(v)* to prepare

grow *(v)* to become bigger

1 The _____ boy gained 5 kilograms in three months.

2 _____ foods do not have many nutrients.

nutrient *(n)* something that is good for the body

3 We are all friends with the _____ man.

4 The _____ object in the sky is a UFO.

object *(n)* a thing

5 My _____ foot really hurts a lot.

6 The _____ baby is in her crib.

crib *(n)* a bed for a baby

7 That person over there looks _____ .

B Combine the sentences by using participles like in the example.

I have to take care of a baby. The baby is crying.

→ *I have to take care of the crying baby.*

1 She lives in the house. It is well-built.

→ _____

well-built *(adj)* made well

2 The train is going fast. It is moving.

→ _____

3 They are members of the team. It is winning.

→ _____

4 I am friends with the boy. He is laughing.

→ _____

5 I know the man in the community. He is respected.

→ _____

respect *(v)* to think highly of

6 Karen has a vase. It is broken.

→ _____

vase *(n)* a container for flowers

7 Mr. Anderson has an office in the building. The building was renovated.

→ _____

renovate *(v)* to repair or improve a building or place

Grammar Plus⁺

Use participles in short phrases. They act like clauses in sentences. Participle phrases should always be next to the noun or pronoun they modify.

▸ The teacher *talking to the students* looks happy.
▸ I mailed the letter *written by my brother*.
▸ Look at the airplane *flying high in the sky*.

Use participle phrases at the beginnings of sentences as well. After these phrases, be sure to insert a comma. Participle phrases describe how the subject in the main clause acts or feels.

▸ *Walking home from school*, Sandra met one of her friends.
▸ *Disappointed by the results*, Peter decided to study harder.
▸ *Interested in English*, Sumi signed up for a class.

Grammar in Action | Fill in the blanks with the words. Then, practice the dialogs with your partner.

1 A You look happy now, Alice.
  B I just had some pie _____ by my mother. It tasted amazing. (make)

2 A You're late for work today, Jeff.
  B _____ to work, I got caught in a huge traffic jam. (drive)
  A You should take the train next time.

3 A Look at the sun _____ over the ocean. (rise)
  B _____ by the beauty, I'm so glad we came here. (surprise)
  A You can say that again.

Chapter Overview

Review the information you learned in this unit.

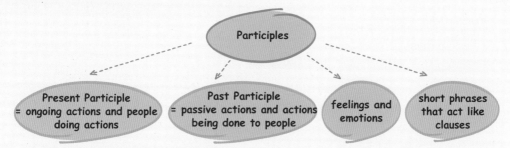

Participles

Present Participle = ongoing actions and people doing actions

Past Participle = passive actions and actions being done to people

feelings and emotions

short phrases that act like clauses

I made it **myself** this morning. (Pronouns)

◀)) 14

Conversation | Listen carefully to the pronouns in the conversation.

A I am hungry. Let's go to your home and eat lunch.

B Actually, I brought my lunch with me. I made it **myself** this morning.

A I didn't bring mine with me because I forgot it.

Grammar Focus

① Use pronouns as substitutes for nouns or noun phrases. There are many types of pronouns.

	Subject Pronoun	Object Pronoun	Possessive Adjective	Possessive Pronoun	Reflexive Pronoun
First Person Singular	I	me	my	mine	myself
Second Person Singular	you	you	your	yours	yourself
Third Person Singular	he/she/it	him/her/it	his/her/its	his/hers	himself/herself/itself
First Person Plural	we	us	our	ours	ourselves
Second Person Plural	you	you	your	yours	yourselves
Third Person Plural	they	them	their	theirs	themselves

② Use subject pronouns as the subjects of sentences and object pronouns as the objects of sentences. In addition, use object pronouns after prepositions.

▸ **I** talk to **her** at work every day.

▸ Ms. Rodgers eats with **them** on Friday.

③ Use possessive adjectives in front of the nouns they modify. Use possessive pronouns alone without any nouns.

▸ **My** name is Eric Johnson.   ▸ Sue has some books. The books are **hers**.

▸ **Their** head office is in New York.   ▸ We live in a big house. The house is **ours**.

④ Use reflexive pronouns to refer to the subject of the sentence because the subject of the action is also either the direct or indirect object.

▸ I asked **myself** a question out loud.

▸ Playing soccer, the boys hurt **themselves**.

💬 **Let's check!** Read each sentence and mark O if it is correct and X if it is incorrect.

1 We like all of our friends.   [   ]   3 I have an umbrella. It is my.   [   ]

2 Peter taught themselves math.   [   ]   4 We gave him some presents for his birthday.   [   ]

Exercise 1

A Read the sentences. Write "S" if the underlined pronoun is a subject pronoun or "O" if the underlined pronoun is an object pronoun.

1 _____ Please tell <u>him</u> about the party this weekend.

2 _____ I talked to Stephanie, and <u>she</u> told me the problem.

3 _____ <u>I</u> want to know the answer to my question.

4 _____ Mr. Roberts invited <u>us</u> to his home tonight.

5 _____ The dog lost the bone. <u>It</u> is looking for the bone.

look for *(v)* to try to find

B Choose the correct possessive adjective or possessive pronoun for each sentence.

1 That book is Steve's, but this one is (my / mine).

2 The drivers all locked the doors of (their / theirs) vehicles.

3 Emily forgot (her / hers) backpack. That one is (her / hers).

4 (Our / Ours) job is to solve the problem.

5 Here is a present for you. This is (your / yours).

vehicle *(n)* anything that moves and carries people or things

C Write the correct reflexive pronouns in the blanks.

1 You _____ asked the best question at the meeting.

2 We taught _____ how to drive a car.

3 Ms. Hampton _____ cooked all of the food.

4 They have burdened _____ with a high mortgage.

5 Mr. Reynolds _____ fixed the broken television.

burden *(v)* to trouble

mortgage *(n)* a loan taken out to buy a house

broken *(adj)* not working properly

Switch It Up!

Read the sentences out loud by yourself or with a partner. Replace the underlined words with pronouns when you speak.

1 Mr. Jacobs talked to <u>the boys</u> today.

2 <u>That woman</u> is sitting by herself on a bench.

3 <u>The workers</u> are taking a training course now.

4 <u>My sister and I</u> are walking to the pharmacy.

5 Somebody is talking to <u>Mr. Anderson</u> on the phone.

6 Please ask <u>Ms. Harper</u> for some advice.

Exercise II

A Correct the underlined parts.

1 Please help <u>mine</u> solve this problem.

2 John had a big problem. He found <u>his</u> in a difficult situation.

3 The house by the lake is <u>hers</u> house.

4 Jason cannot find <u>he</u> favorite T-shirt.

5 The students taught <u>their</u> soccer.

6 This car is Tina's. That car is not <u>she</u>.

7 <u>Us</u> remembered to turn off the lights.

B Choose the best options for the sentences.

1 I want to visit my grandparents in _____ hometown.
   a. me   b. their   c. mine   d. theirs

2 They are helping _____ to more food.
   a. herself   b. himself   c. themselves   d. yourself

3 You should not bring _____ dog in here.
   a. your   b. you   c. yours   d. yourself

4 I saw that boy playing with the toys. They are certainly _____ .
   a. he   b. him   c. himself   d. his

5 Ms. McCloud drives _____ car to work.
   a. her   b. hers   c. she   d. herself

6 Can you please tell _____ your phone number?
   a. me   b. myself   c. my   d. mine

7 The birds are sleeping in _____ nests.
   a. their   b. them   c. its   d. it

hometown *(n)* the place where a person is from or grew up

help oneself *(v)* to make an effort for oneself

bring *(v)* to take

Grammar Plus⁺

Use **it** as an impersonal pronoun. You can use **it** as the subject for an impersonal verb. Use **it** as an impersonal pronoun to talk about the weather, the day, the time, and the date.

▸ **It** is snowing right now.

▸ **It** is three thirty in the afternoon.

▸ **It** is Saturday morning.

▸ **It** is July 16.

Use **it** as the subject of a sentence when the real subject is an infinitive. Use this form because starting the sentence with an infinitive would read unnaturally.

▸ **It** is fun <u>to watch</u> cartoons. (NOT "To watch cartoons is fun.")

▸ **It** was great <u>to see</u> you again. (NOT "To see you again was great.")

▸ **It** is interesting <u>to read</u> this book. (NOT "To read this book is interesting.")

Grammar in Action | Fill in the blanks with the correct words. Then, practice the dialogs with your partner.

1 A Hello. _____ is nice to meet you.

  B _____ is a pleasure _____ you, too. (meet)

2 A It is exciting _____ board games. (play)

  B When _____ is raining, I play them with my friends.

  A _____ might rain soon. Shall we play a board game?

3 A _____ is so hard _____ math. Don't you agree? (learn)

  B Actually, it is pretty easy. Do you want me to teach you?

  A Yes, I do. _____ would be wonderful to get better at math.

Chapter Overview

Review the information you learned in this unit.

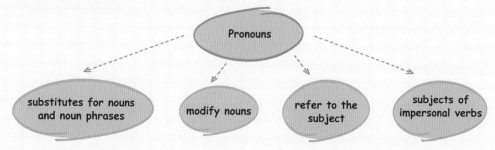

Pronouns

substitutes for nouns and noun phrases

modify nouns

refer to the subject

subjects of impersonal verbs

I'm visiting **a few countries** in Europe.

(Countable/Uncountable Nouns and Articles)

🔊 15

Conversation | Listen carefully to the countable nouns, the uncountable nouns, and the articles in the conversation.

A I'm visiting **a few countries** in Europe next week.

B That sounds fun. Are you going to France?

A Yes, I am. I'm visiting France, Italy, Spain, and Greece.

Grammar Focus

① Countable nouns can be counted, so they have a plural form and can take singular or plural verbs. Uncountable nouns cannot be counted, so they have no plural form and can only take singular verbs.

Countable Nouns	Uncountable Nouns
an apple / 2 apples / 3 apples a car / 5 cars / 10 cars a man / 4 men / 8 men	air, sugar, salt, rice, water, milk, juice, coffee, butter, information, equipment, furniture, money, baggage, luggage, peace, love, success, happiness, news...
A boy *rides* on the bus. **Three computers** *are* on the desk.	The **air** *is* hard to breathe here. My **luggage** *costs* a lot of money.

② Use **a** or **an** the first time you mention a noun and to name a member of a group, to mean one, and to state expressions that quantify.

▸ I want to borrow **a** pen.

▸ That woman is **an** engineer.

▸ He would like **a** sandwich.

▸ They have **a** lot of money.

③ Use **the** the second time you mention a noun and to define something, to indicate there is just one of something, and to describe a unique thing. You can also use it before some proper nouns, such as oceans, rivers, and mountain ranges.

▸ He has a car. I want to ride in **the** car.

▸ **The** sun is a star.

▸ Let's go to **the** hospital.

▸ She is sailing on **the** Han River.

④ Use the zero article (ø) to talk about things in general, to mention countries, meals, and languages, to state people's names and titles, and to name specific mountains, lakes, islands, and most cities.

▸ We often play **soccer** after school.

▸ **Mr. Horner** is my friend.

▸ They eat **lunch** at 12:00.

▸ His uncle lives in **Paris**.

💬 **Let's check!** Read each sentence and mark O if it is correct and X if it is incorrect.

1 Please lend me some moneys. [ ]

2 Ms. Jenkins is a teacher. [ ]

3 He flew across Atlantic Ocean. [ ]

4 Five women are talking together. [ ]

Exercise 1

A Complete the sentences with *a*, *an*, *the*, or ø.

1 Millions of people live in _____ Los Angeles.

2 The rocket is flying to _____ moon.

3 Do you know how to speak _____ Russian?

4 I can see _____ cat in a tree.

5 There is _____ lot of money in the wallet.

6 _____ Alps are mountains in Europe.

7 There is _____ airplane in the sky.

wallet *(n)* a small folding pocketbook for carrying money and cards

B Complete the sentences with the words in the box by changing them into their correct forms. Then, change the verbs in parentheses to their singular or plural forms.

lion	person	dog	rice	pollution	travel	gasoline

pollution *(n)* harmful substances in the air, ground, or water

1 The air _____ in the city (be) very bad.

2 There (be) many _____ at the zoo.

3 _____ (be) needed to make the car run.

4 A lot of _____ (be) waiting in line at the theater.

5 _____ to other countries (have) become very popular.

6 _____ (taste) good to many people around the world.

7 Several _____ (live) in the house across the street.

run *(v)* to operate

Switch It Up!

Write "C" for countable or "U" for uncountable for each of the following words.

1	bread		9	flour		17	partner	
2	ticket		10	employee		18	furniture	
3	subway		11	salt		19	body	
4	transportation		12	ocean		20	information	
5	horse		13	machine		21	happiness	
6	makeup		14	vehicle		22	star	
7	computer		15	rain		23	clothing	
8	baggage		16	hair		24	friend	

Exercise II

Correct the underlined parts.

1 We visited <u>the</u> Rome last summer vacation.

2 The <u>airs</u> in the mountains smells good.

3 Ken put <u>salts</u> and pepper on his food.

4 <u>The</u> Mr. Morris is 42 years old.

5 There are two <u>orange</u> in the box.

6 I poured some <u>milks</u> in my coffee.

7 The farmer has three <u>horse</u> on his farm.

8 <u>The</u> Mexico is located by the Pacific Ocean.

9 Please give me a <u>pencils</u>.

10 Some astronauts went to <u>moon</u>.

11 The engineer will repair the <u>equipments</u>.

12 He poured a lot of water in <u>swimming pool</u>.

13 We will eat <u>a</u> sandwiches for lunch.

14 She packed five shirts in her <u>luggages</u>.

15 She will move to <u>a</u> London next year.

16 You need to add <u>sugars</u> to make cookies.

17 Joe has <u>coin</u> in his pocket.

18 They want to climb <u>the</u> Mt. Everest.

pour *(v)* to move a liquid from one place to another

be located *(v)* to be found in a certain place

astronaut *(n)* a person who goes into space

equipment *(n)* anything used for a certain purpose

pack *(v)* to put something into a bag

luggage *(n)* a suitcase

Grammar Plus⁺

Use **there is** and **there are** to say that something exists. Use **there is** with singular countable nouns and uncountable nouns. Use **there are** with plural countable nouns.

▶ **There is** *some sugar* in the bowl.   ▶ **There are** *three men* in the room.

Use the quantifiers **many** and **a few** with countable nouns and **much** and a **little** with uncountable nouns. Use **some** with countable and uncountable nouns in affirmative statements and questions and **any** with countable and uncountable nouns in negative statements and questions.

▶ David has **many** *friends*.   ▶ David does not spend **much** *money*.

▶ Janet buys **a few** *books*.   ▶ Janet has **little** *time*.

▶ He has **some** *sandwiches* and *milk* for lunch.   ▶ He doesn't have **any** *cookies* or *bread*.

*Use **much** in questions and negative statements. For affirmative statements, use an adverb such as *very* with **much** or **much** with a comparative adjective.

I have **much** money. (X)   I have *very* **much** money. (O)   I have **much** *more* money. (O)

Grammar in Action | Fill in the blanks with the words you learned above. Then, practice the dialogs with your partner.

1 A _____ is a delicious smell coming from the kitchen.

   B I cooked _____ chicken and rice for dinner.

2 A Excuse me, but do you have _____ time?

   B Well, I don't have _____ time. What do you need?

   A There are several bags. Can you help me carry _____ to the office?

3 A I want to buy _____ books. Can I borrow some money?

   B Sorry, but I don't have _____ bills. I only have _____ coins.

   A Oh, I can get _____ money from the machine over there.

Chapter Overview

Review the information you learned in this unit.

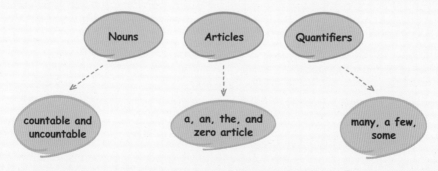

Nouns → countable and uncountable

Articles → a, an, the, and zero article

Quantifiers → many, a few, some

16 I think it's **really boring**. (Adjectives and Adverbs)

🔊 16

Conversation | Listen carefully to the adjectives and adverbs in the conversation.

A I love this TV show. It's so funny.

B Seriously? I think it's **really boring**.

A I watch it every time it's on TV.

B I prefer watching sporting events. They are exciting to me.

Grammar Focus

① Adjectives modify nouns, noun phrases, and pronouns. They describe these words. They usually come before the word or words they modify. But they can also follow the *be* verb.

- ▸ John is a **smart** *man*.
- ▸ The book *is* **interesting**.
- ▸ This is a **fun** *video game*.
- ▸ His idea *is* **creative**.

Adverbs modify verbs, adjectives, or other adverbs. They answer questions such as *when, where, why, how,* and *to what extent.*

- ▸ "*How* are the children walking?" "The children *are walking* **slowly**."
- ▸ "*Why* is that object hard to carry?" "It is **really** *heavy*."

② Adjectives and adverbs often have similar forms. In many cases, you can add **-ly** or **-ily** to the end of an adjective to create an adverb.

quick – quick**ly**	serious – serious**ly**	kind – kind**ly**	usual – usual**ly**	nice – nice**ly**	bad – bad**ly**
angry – angr**ily**	heavy – heav**ily**	easy – eas**ily**	slow – slow**ly**	real – real**ly**	fair – fair**ly**

③ Some adjectives and adverbs have the same form. These include words such as **hard, early, free, late, long, fast, wide,** and **high.**

Adjective	Adverb
Computer programming can be **hard**.	Dana works **hard** every day.
I had a **late** night yesterday.	He arrived **late** for the party.
Allen drives a **fast** car.	A plane can fly **fast**.
This is a **high** fence.	The boy jumped **high**.

④ Use **good** as an adjective but **well** as an adverb.

- ▸ Irene is a **good** worker.
- ▸ This gold ring looks **good**.
- ▸ I do not feel **well** now.
- ▸ The team played **well** during the game.

💬 **Let's check!** Read each sentence and mark O if it is correct and X if it is incorrect.

1 Some animals can run fast. [　]　　**3** The food she cooked tasted nice. [　]

2 Carla looks like a very seriously woman. [　]　　**4** The man yelled angry at the young boys. [　]

Exercise 1

A Circle the correct words for the sentences.

1 The big computer box feels (heavy / heavily).

2 The (slow / slowly) tortoise won the race against the hare.

3 Andrea cooked the food very (good / well) last night.

4 The businessman spoke (angry / angrily) to the customer.

5 Ms. Watson (usual / usually) wakes up early in the morning.

6 The police arrested the (bad / badly) man and sent him to jail.

7 She is a (kind / kindly) old woman, so everyone likes her.

B Complete the sentences with the words in the box.

| boring   well   happily   seriously   nice   swift   really |

1 Nobody wanted to read the _____ book.

2 Brad is _____ , so he has a lot of friends.

3 The movie was _____ funny, so everyone laughed a lot.

4 Sue smiled _____ during her birthday party.

5 The test was hard, so nobody did _____ on it.

6 The _____ plane arrived at its destination on time.

7 Mr. Johnson talked _____ with his wife.

businessman (n) a man who works at a company

customer (n) a shopper at a store

early (adv) before an appointed time

arrest (v) to catch and hold a person

jail (n) a place where criminals spend time

laugh (v) to make a loud sound to show amusement

Switch It Up!

Read the following directions to play bingo with your group.

1 Choose nine adjectives and adverbs from the first two pages of the unit.

2 Write them in the squares on the right.

3 Take turns saying a word in English and also saying its meaning in your native language.

4 The first person to cross out all nine squares is the winner.

Exercise 11

A Correct the underlined parts.

1 The rules of the game are <u>fairily</u> easy to understand.

2 Some people are able to learn new languages <u>fastly</u>.

3 Everyone agreed the movie was <u>real</u> boring.

4 They had a <u>funnily</u> time at the birthday party.

5 I wrote <u>slow</u> to avoid making any mistakes.

6 There is a <u>highly</u> building in the middle of the city.

7 The race is very <u>longly</u>, so it takes a while to finish.

agree *(v)* to say that someone is right about something

make a mistake *(v)* to do something wrong or bad

take a while *(v)* to take a long time to do something

finish *(v)* to complete

B Complete the crossword puzzle. Change the adjectives into adverbs if necessary.

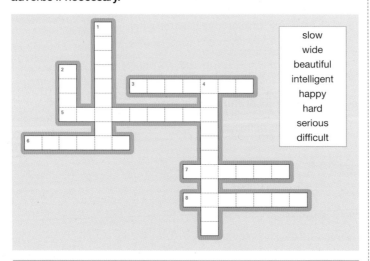

slow
wide
beautiful
intelligent
happy
hard
serious
difficult

serious *(adj)* relating to deep thought

Across

3 David sings _____ while driving to work.
5 It is _____ for me to dance in public.
6 It is not good for people to work too _____.
7 Harry has traveled _____ for the past few years.
8 She has a very _____ look on her face.

Down

1 Marilyn is wearing a _____ white sweater.
2 The actors practiced _____ before the performance.
4 The _____ student got a perfect score on the test.

in public *(adv)* in front of other people

practice *(v)* to do something many times in order to improve

Grammar Plus⁺

Some adjectives end in **-ly**. These include **friendly, ugly, silly, chilly, lonely,** and **lovely.** These words do not have adverb forms. To use them like adverbs, you must change the form of the sentence.

▸ He was acting **sillyly**. (X)   He was acting **in a silly way**. (O)

▸ She spoke **friendlyly** to everyone. (X)   She spoke **in a friendly manner** to everyone. (O)

Some adverbs are not formed from adjectives. These include **very, too, just, so, quite,** and **soon.**

▸ It is raining **very** hard now.

▸ Someone **just** arrived in the office.

▸ Please finish your work on this project **soon**.

*Very means "a lot." **Too** means "more than there should be."

Grammar in Action | Fill in the blanks with the words you learned above. Then, practice the dialogs with your partner.

1 A How do you feel living by yourself?

    B It's all right, but I feel _____ sometimes.

2 A How was the comedy show?

    B It was great. The comedian spoke in a _____ voice.

    A It sounds _____ funny. I bet you had a lot of fun.

3 A Look at this present I got for my birthday.

    B It's _____ . Who gave it to you?

    A My friend Tracy. We are _____ close to each other.

Chapter Overview

Review the information you learned in this unit.

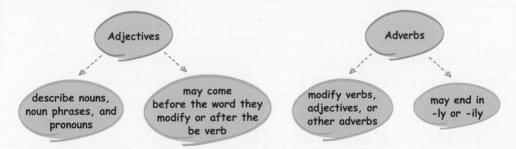

Adjectives
- describe nouns, noun phrases, and pronouns
- may come before the word they modify or after the be verb

Adverbs
- modify verbs, adjectives, or other adverbs
- may end in -ly or -ily

17 It tastes **more delicious**. (Comparisons)

◀)) 17

Conversation | Listen carefully to the comparisons in the conversation.

A How do you like this cake? Does it taste better than the cherry pie?

B It's not as sweet as the cherry pie. But it tastes **more delicious**.

A Great. The cake was harder to make than the pie.

Grammar Focus

① Make comparative/superlative adjectives like this:

words with one or two syllables ending with -y, -er, -ow, -le, or most consonants	
adjective + -er	slower, kinder, blacker, sooner, narrower, longer, lighter
adjective + -est	slowest, kindest, blackest, soonest, narrowest, longest, lightest
words with a silent -e at the end	
adjective + -r	nicer, later, simpler, politer, closer, rarer
adjective + -st	nicest, latest, simplest, politest, closest, rarest
words ending in -y	
adjective + -ier (remove the -y)	prettier, happier, fancier, angrier, busier
adjective + -iest (remove the -y)	prettiest, happiest, fanciest, angriest, busiest
short words with little stress on the vowel	
adjective + double consonant + -er	wetter, hotter, madder, flatter
adjective + double consonant + -est	wettest, hottest, maddest, flattest
most words longer than two syllables	
more + adjective	more handsome, more intelligent, more interesting
(the) most + adjective	(the) most handsome, (the) most intelligent, (the) most interesting

② Use comparative adjectives to compare or contrast two people, places, things, or ideas. You often use *than* when making a comparison. Use superlative adjectives to compare or contrast three or more people, places, things, or ideas.

▸ The dog is **faster** *than* the cat.   ▸ David is **the smartest** student in his class.

▸ I cook **better** *than* you.   ▸ Helen studies **the hardest** of the three girls.

💬 **Let's check!** Read each sentence and mark O if it is correct and X if it is incorrect.

1 Doug is funier than his friend.   [   ]   **3** Amy is the most beautifulest girl in the class. [   ]

2 Math is more interesting than science.   [   ]   **4** He owns the rarest painting of all.   [   ]

Exercise I

A Circle the correct answer.

1 Earth is (farther / the farthest) from the sun than Mercury.

far *(adj)* at a great distance from

2 A sports car is (more expensive / the most expensive) than a motorcycle.

3 Greg is (taller / the tallest) player on the basketball team.

4 Cherries taste (better / the best) than oranges.

5 (Faster / The fastest) runner will win the race.

6 The elephant is (larger / the largest) of all animals.

7 David is (more famous / the most famous) movie star in the world.

famous *(adj)* very well known

B Complete the sentences with the words in parentheses. Change the forms of the words.

1 Mary's room looks _____ than Charles's room. (clean)

2 A rocket can fly _____ than an airplane. (fast)

3 Today is _____ day of the entire year. (hot)

entire *(adj)* whole; complete

4 Who is _____ man in the movie? (handsome)

5 Mark is _____ than his friend John. (old)

6 Janet is _____ than her sister. (intelligent)

7 There are three bags, and this one is _____ . (heavy)

Switch It Up!

Look at the pictures. Then, compare and contrast the items in the pictures by using the presented words.

1 tall	2 long	3 dangerous

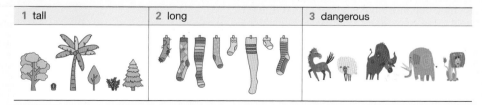

The first tree is taller than the second one...

Exercise 11

A Complete the sentences with the words in the box. Use the words in their comparative or superlative forms.

fast	happy	polite	nice	expensive	wet	beautiful

1 Email is _____ than regular mail.

2 The prices are high. This restaurant is _____ one in town.

3 It is raining a lot. August is _____ month in summer.

4 Steve has good manners. He is _____ than his friend.

5 The model is _____ woman in the room.

6 I got an A+ on the test. My friend got a C. I feel _____ than my friend.

7 Sue is so kind. She is _____ person I know.

regular *(adj)* normal

town *(n)* a small city

manners *(n)* ways of behaving politely

B Correct the underlined parts.

1 Today is <u>clouder</u> than yesterday.

2 We took the <u>difficultest</u> test this morning.

3 Winter is <u>coldier</u> than fall.

4 She owns the <u>most cute</u> dog in the world.

5 A monkey's arms are <u>hairer</u> than a person's.

6 A mouse is smaller <u>to</u> a horse.

7 Rock music sounds <u>loud</u> than classical music.

8 He is the most <u>handsomest</u> man in the film.

9 My friend is <u>more funny</u> than the comedian.

cloudy *(adj)* having lots of clouds in the sky

own *(v)* to have or possess

hairy *(adj)* having a large amount of hair

loud *(adj)* making a strong sound

classical *(adj)* relating to a sophisticated style

Grammar Plus⁺

Use **as . . . as** to indicate that two things are the same as each other. Put an adjective between **as** and **as**. Use **not as . . . as** to indicate that two things are different from each other.

▸ John is **as old as** his twin brother.　▸ Bubble gum is **not as expensive as** a candy bar.

▸ Mary studies **as hard as** her friend Tina.　▸ The baby is **not as tall as** his sister.

Use **less + adjective** to make a contrast between two people, places, things, or ideas. Use **the least + adjective** to make a contrast between three or more people, places, things, or ideas.

▸ This book is **less interesting** than that one.　▸ She is **the least bored** of the three people.

▸ A horse is **less big** than a hippo.　▸ Kevin is **the least busy** of all the students.

Grammar in Action | Fill in the blanks with the words you learned above. Then, practice the dialogs with your partner.

1 A Look at Gerald. He is ＿＿＿＿＿ tall ＿＿＿＿＿ Mark.

   B No, he is ＿＿＿＿＿ tall than Mark.

2 A I am ＿＿＿＿＿ successful than I was in the past.

   B Maybe you are ＿＿＿＿＿ working ＿＿＿＿＿ hard ＿＿＿＿＿ you did before.

   A No, it's not that. The economy is ＿＿＿＿＿ healthy in the past five years.

3 A Science-fiction novels are ＿＿＿＿＿ fun ＿＿＿＿＿ fantasy novels.

   B I find fantasy novels ＿＿＿＿＿ interesting than science-fiction novels. But I love detective stories.

   A No way. They are ＿＿＿＿＿ exciting as science-fiction novels.

Chapter Overview

Review the information you learned in this unit.

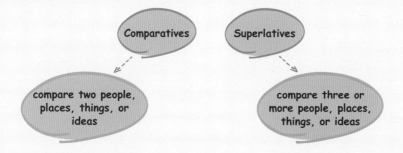

Comparatives — compare two people, places, things, or ideas

Superlatives — compare three or more people, places, things, or ideas

The woman **that** is singing is my cousin.

(Relative Clauses I)

◀)) 18

Conversation | Listen carefully to the relative clauses in the conversation.

A Look at that woman who is singing on stage. Do you know who she is?

B The woman **that** is singing is my cousin. She wrote that song.

A I'm really impressed. You have many talented family members.

B Wait for the next act. It's my brother, who will perform some magic tricks.

Grammar Focus

Use relative pronouns to connect two sentences to each other. Relative pronouns such as **who**, **whom**, **that**, and **which** refer to the noun mentioned before them.

Who(m) (people)
John is a man. John has a job. → John is a man **who** has a job. Allison likes her house. Allison lives in Seattle. → Allison, **who** lives in Seattle, likes her house. George can speak Chinese. Everyone likes George. → George, **who(m)** everyone likes, can speak Chinese.
That (people or things)
David is a student. David studies hard. → David is a student **that** studies hard. Thomas bought a shirt. The shirt is blue. → The shirt **that** Thomas bought is blue. The sun is a star. The sun is the center of the solar system. → The sun is a star **that** is the center of the solar system.
Which (anything that is not a person)
I have a key. The key opens the door. → I have a key **which** opens the door. The dog bit the man. The dog was growling. → The dog, **which** was growling, bit the man. Roses are flowers. Roses smell nice. → Roses, **which** smell nice, are flowers.

Use a comma before a relative pronoun and after the relative clause when the information is not important to understanding the meaning of the independent clause.

Never use a comma before **that** when it is used as a relative pronoun.

💬 **Let's check!** Read each sentence and mark O if it is correct and X if it is incorrect.

1 Eric is the man who is helping us.　　　[　]
3 The teacher whom we know is coming into the room. [　]

2 Joanie, which is a student, is really nice. [　]
4 Mr. Johnson, that is a lawyer, is always busy.　　[　]

Exercise 1

A Correct the underlined parts.

1 Mark, <u>whom</u> is twenty years old, has a girlfriend.

2 The tea, <u>is which</u> hot, tastes great.

3 Nobody knew the woman <u>which</u> was with Karen.

4 The sofa, <u>that</u> is made of leather, costs a lot.

leather (n) the preserved skin of an animal

cost (v) to require payment for

5 This is the printer <u>who</u> makes color copies.

6 The doctor <u>which</u> you prefer is busy now.

prefer (v) to like one thing more than another

7 This meal, <u>whom</u> is seafood, is very expensive.

B Complete the sentences with the endings in the box. Choose the correct relative pronoun for each ending.

is worth a lot of money   works at that company   was really fun
cooked your dinner   we all knew   breaks down very often

break down (v) to stop working properly

often (adv) frequently

1 I know a businessman _____ .

2 Susan has a car _____ .

3 He will buy a gold ring _____ .

4 Martin is the chef _____ .

chef (n) a cook

5 We recognized the movie star _____ .

recognize (v) to see a person and to know who it is

6 They played a game _____ .

Switch It Up!

Look at the sentences below. Then, complete them with your own ideas. Be sure to use the correct relative pronouns.

My bedroom is the place *that I love the most.*

1 My best friend is the person . . .

2 2019 was the year . . .

3 I remember the trip . . .

4 I love food . . .

5 I like people . . .

Exercise II

A Combine the sentences by using the relative pronouns in parentheses.

1 I love this song. The song is called *Home Again*. (which)

2 The man has a car. The car can go fast. (that)

3 The bus driver is smiling. The bus driver is an old man. (who)

4 You met Ms. Johnson. You are related to Ms. Johnson. (whom)

related *(adj)* connected to

5 The calculator is broken. I bought the calculator. (that)

calculator *(n)* a handheld machine that can do math problems

6 She recalls the man. The man saved her life. (who)

recall *(v)* to remember

7 I earned some money. I spent all of the money. (which)

earn *(v)* to make money

B Use the words to make sentences with relative pronouns.

1 was / we / the game / exciting / that / remember

2 my favorite books / love / are / I / novels / which

3 a Shi-tzu / the dog / is / is / running / which

4 Mr. Hampton / a trip / whom / respect / is taking / we

take a trip *(v)* to travel

5 a hospital / who / a nurse / my sister / works / at / is

work *(v)* to be successful

6 that / well / I / an idea / work / should / have

7 a sport / play / soccer / which / many / is / children

Grammar Plus⁺

Use **whose** when showing possession for people, animals, or things.

▸ Jane is the person **whose** pencil I borrowed.

▸ The elephant, **whose** body is huge, is the largest land animal.

▸ We went to the building, **whose** front door was locked.

Use **whoever** when the relative pronoun is the subject of the relative clause. Use **whomever** when the relative pronoun is the object of the relative clause. Use **whoever** and **whomever** when the identity of the person being referred to is unknown or does not matter.

▸ I want to meet **whoever** cooked this pie.

▸ Talk to **whomever** you want to go on the trip with.

▸ She can help **whoever** needs assistance.

Grammar in Action | Fill in the blanks with the words you learned above. Then, practice the dialogs with your partner.

1 A This picture looks nice. Who made it?

 B Steve did it. He is the artist _____ paintings look the best.

2 A Who are we going to hire for the job?

 B Let's hire _____ we think does the best at the interview.

 A That's an idea which should work. I'll speak with _____ is conducting the interviews.

3 A I just found a wallet. It was lying on the ground.

 B We need to figure out _____ lost it.

 A Wait. I just looked. It is Tom _____ wallet I just found.

Chapter Overview

Review the information you learned in this unit.

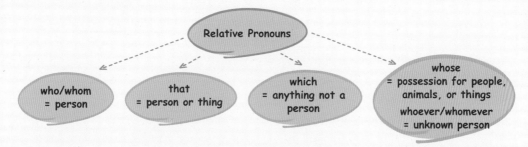

It's at 5:30 **when** the first performer will go on stage. (Relative Clauses II)

🔊 19

Conversation | Listen carefully to the relative clauses in the conversation.

A Brenda, do you remember when the concert starts?

B Yes, I do. It's at 5:30 **when** the first performer will go on stage.

A Is that the reason why you are getting ready to leave work?

B That's right. We need to leave soon to find a parking place.

Grammar Focus

① Use relative adverbs to connect two sentences to each other. Relative adverbs such as **where**, **when**, and **why** refer to the noun mentioned before them.

where	to refer to a place	Amy went to Paris, **where** she is studying now.
when	to refer to a time	September is the month **when** Sue has her birthday.
why	to refer to a reason	Irene told Eric the reason **why** she was so happy.
how	to refer to a manner, method, or way	Please tell me **how** you solved the problem.

② It is common to use expressions such as *the place, the time, the day,* and *the reason* before relative adverbs.

▸ This is *the place* **where** I was born.

▸ 12:00 is *the time* **when** most people eat lunch.

▸ Joe remembers *the day* **when** he met his wife.

▸ Do you know *the reason* **why** the bus stopped?

▸ Susan told her mother **how** she would pay for college.

③ Do not use a comma before a relative adverb when the information is important to understanding the meaning of the independent clause. Use a comma before a relative adverb and after the relative clause when the information is not important to understanding the meaning of the independent clause.

▸ I remember August, **when** it rained every day.

▸ Let's sit at this table, **where** we will all be comfortable.

▸ The restaurant, **where** we had lunch, is closing.

💬 **Let's check!** Read each sentence and mark O if it is correct and X if it is incorrect.

1 Do you know the time where the meeting begins? [   ] **3** State the day why the interview is. [   ]

2 I remember the reason why she quit the team. [   ] **4** Please explain how we can play this game. [   ]

Exercise I

A Circle the correct words.

1 The reason (where / **why**) Janet likes Tom is simple.

2 Please explain to us (**how** / where) you can fix the machine.

3 We can shop at the store (which / **where**) you bought the scarf.

4 Nobody knows the reason (**why** / how) David is late.

5 This is the time (**when** / where) people like to go home.

6 I will ask Mark (**what** / why) he is moving.

7 The bus stop (**where** / how) I take the bus is one block away.

reason *(n)* a cause for an action or belief

move *(v)* to go to another place to live

B Correct the underlined parts.

1 I know a place <u>which</u> we can relax.

2 James told her <u>when the time</u> the movie starts.

3 Please explain the reason <u>what</u> dinner is not ready.

4 The teacher described <u>what</u> the water cycle works.

5 January 1 is the day <u>how</u> people celebrate the new year.

6 Is that the apartment <u>when</u> Stan used to live?

7 In winter, <u>why</u> the weather is cold, people go skiing.

water cycle *(n)* the process through which water changes forms on the Earth

celebrate *(v)* to observe a special day by doing various events

used to *(v)* to have done something in the past but not doing it anymore

Switch It Up!

Look at the sentences. Then, complete them with your own ideas. Be sure to use the correct relative pronouns.

I remember the time *when we watched a movie together.*

1 I want you to explain . . .

2 December is the month . . .

3 This restaurant is the place . . .

4 I remember the reason . . .

Exercise 11

A Match the sentences.

1 Peter mentioned to Sam   [   ]

2 Please explain to me   [   ]

3 Chris thinks the time   [   ]

4 I remember the reason   [   ]

5 This is the field   [   ]

6 They ate at a restaurant   [   ]

7 That was the day   [   ]

> a. why John doesn't like scary movies.
> b. when they are meeting is fine.
> c. how you will solve the puzzle.
> d. why he wanted to travel abroad.
> e. where the food is very expensive.
> f. when Susan went to the hair salon.
> g. where we play soccer.

mention *(v)* say something about it, usually briefly

field *(n)* an area of grass where sports are played

scary *(adj)* frightening

abroad *(adv)* going to a foreign country, usually one which is separated from the country where you live by an ocean or a sea

B Combine the sentences by using the relative adverbs in parentheses.

1 We are going to the theater. The movie is playing there. (where)

2 Please state the time. The game starts at that time. (when)

3 We are going home. She often asks us. (how)

4 The hotel is expensive. We stayed at the hotel. (where)

5 It is in summer. There is a lot of rain. (when)

6 I failed the test. I remember the reason. (why)

7 The beach is popular with people. Sue lives near the beach. (where)

state *(v)* to say out loud

ask *(v)* to make a question

stay *(v)* to remain somewhere for a while

fail *(v)* to do very badly on or at

near *(prep)* close to

Grammar Plus⁺

Use **in which** or **at which** to replace **where** as a relative adverb. Use **in which** or **on which** to replace **when** as a relative adverb. Use **for which** to replace **why** as a relative adverb.

▸ The house **where** Tina lives is next door.
  → The house **in which** Tina lives is next door.
▸ This is the restaurant **where** we will have lunch.
  → This is the restaurant **at which** we will have lunch.
▸ This is the day **when** we celebrate her birthday.
  → This is the day **on which** we celebrate her birthday.
▸ What is the year **when** you were born?
  → What is the year **in which** you were born?
▸ I know the reason **why** Nancy forgot to study.
  → I know the reason **for which** Nancy forgot to study.

Grammar in Action | Fill in the blanks with the words you learned above. Then, practice the dialogs with your partner.

1 **A** I'd like to know the name of a store _____ I can buy a laptop.
  B Go to the next street. You can find a great store there.

2 **A** Nobody knows the reason _____ Chris went home early.
  B I believe he is meeting a client at the café _____ he often goes.

3 **A** 1985 is the year _____ our company was founded.
  B Do you know the reason _____ Mr. Sampson started it?
  A Yes, I do. He wanted to help people invest their money.

Chapter Overview

Review the information you learned in this unit.

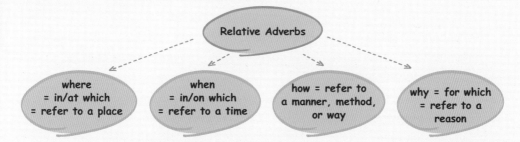

Relative Adverbs

where
= in/at which
= refer to a place

when
= in/on which
= refer to a time

how = refer to
a manner, method,
or way

why = for which
= refer to a
reason

How much does it cost? (Wh-Questions)

◀)) 20

Conversation | Listen carefully to the wh-question words in the conversation.

A Look at these two jackets. Which one do you prefer?

B I like the black one. **How** much does it cost?

A It costs $50. What do you think of the other one?

B It looks good on you. I think you should buy it.

Grammar Focus

① Ask questions with wh-question words like this:

wh-question word + do/does + subject + verb	**Where** does your brother work?
wh-question word + be + subject	**When** is the movie?

② Use wh-question words to ask about the following:

who	person	**Who** do you like?
what	thing	**What** is that?
when	time	**When** does the game start?
where	location	**Where** do you live?
how	directions	**How** does he know the answer?
why	reason	**Why** is this answer wrong?
which	choice	**Which** do you prefer, the green one or the blue one?

③ Use **do** or **does** to ask questions with wh-question words. But do not use **do** or **does** in the answers in affirmative statements.

  ▶ "*What* **do** you **want** for dinner?" "I **want** chicken." / "I **don't want** spaghetti."

  ▶ "*Where* **does** Ms. Johnson **work**?" "She **works** in Seoul." / "She **doesn't have** a job."

  ▶ "*Which* **do** you **like**?" "I **like** the first one." / "I **don't like** either one."

④ Use **be** or other **auxiliary verbs** to ask questions with wh-question words. Use the same verbs in the answers in affirmative statements and negative responses.

  ▶ "*Where* **is** Molly?" "She **is** on the bus." / "She **isn't** here."

  ▶ "*What* **can** you **speak**?" "I **can speak** French." / "I **can't speak** a foreign language."

  ▶ "*When* **will** you **come** here?" "I **will come** tonight." / "I **won't come** at all."

Let's check! Read each sentence and mark O if it is correct and X if it is incorrect.

1 What do you remember?   [   ]   3 How is your brother doing?   [   ]

2 When does start the movie?   [   ]   4 Where can we meeting tonight?   [   ]

Exercise 1

A Complete the sentences with the words in parentheses.

1 What _____ your name? (be)

2 How _____ this machine _____? (work)

3 Where _____ you _____ school? (attend)

4 When _____ you _____ on a plane next week? (fly)

5 Which _____ Nancy _____ to buy, this one or that one? (want)

6 Who _____ the baby right now? (watch)

7 Why _____ you never _____ on time at work? (arrive)

attend (v) to go to an event

B Complete the sentences with the words in the box.

| Who | When | What | Which | How | Where | Why |

1 _____ do you play this game?

2 _____ does Mr. Hemingway eat for lunch?

3 _____ is he going for vacation?

4 _____ are we inviting to the birthday party?

5 _____ should we take, the first left or the second left?

6 _____ do you always get upset easily?

7 _____ does Mr. Ruth's bus depart from the station?

invite (v) to ask a person to go to an event, place, etc.

upset (adj) unhappy or angry

easily (adv) without any problems

depart (v) to leave

Switch It Up!

Fill in the blanks to complete the following sentences. Then, ask and answer the questions with your partner.

1 What ... ? (food)

2 Who ... ? (best friend)

3 Where ... ? (live)

4 When ... ? (go to bed)

5 Why ... ? (study hard)

6 How ... ? (like English)

7 Which ... ? (prefer, sports, movies)

A *What is your favorite food?* **B** *My favorite food is scrambled eggs.*

Exercise II

A Correct the underlined parts.

1 <u>What they</u> think about the problem?

2 <u>When</u> can work for me tomorrow night?

3 When <u>did</u> you born?

4 Why does he <u>dislikes</u> reading?

dislike *(v)* not to like or enjoy

5 <u>Does which</u> Joe prefer, traveling or staying home?

6 Where shall we <u>going</u> shopping today?

7 How <u>is</u> your mother feel these days?

B Match the sentences.

1 What is the correct answer? [   ]

correct *(adj)* right

2 Where are you going? [   ]

3 When shall we meet? [   ]

4 Who does John work for? [   ]

5 How can I use this machine? [   ]

6 Which are you planning to do? [   ]

7 Why is the window broken? [   ]

broken *(adj)* torn or in pieces

a. Let's meet tonight at 8:00.
b. I hit it with a baseball.
c. He doesn't work for anyone.
d. I can show you.
e. The answer is 17.
f. I'm going home now.
g. I don't know yet.

yet *(adv)* at the present time

Grammar Plus⁺

Add a noun after **what** to ask questions. In most cases, do not include the noun in the answer.

- ▸ "**What time** do you wake up?" "I wake up at 7:30 every day."
- ▸ "**What movie** is she watching?" "She is watching *Jaws*."
- ▸ "**What store** do you shop at?" "I often shop at T-Mart."

Add a noun after **which** to ask questions. Add **much/many + noun** after **how** to ask questions.

- ▸ "**Which dog** is yours?" "The one on the left is mine."
- ▸ "**Which way** are you going?" "I'm taking the highway there."
- ▸ "**How much time** does it take?" "It takes about ten minutes."
- ▸ "**How many pencils** do you have?" "I have three pencils."

Grammar in Action | Fill in the blanks with the words you learned above. Then, practice the dialogs with your partner.

1 A _____ concert did you buy tickets for?
  B I bought tickets for the Screaming Eagles.

2 A Oh, no. I forgot my wallet. _____ money do you have?
  B Why do you need some money?
  A I want to buy some food. Can I borrow some money?

3 A Excuse me. _____ time is it?
  B It's five thirty. Why do you want to know the time?
  A I'm meeting Wendy at 6:00. How long does it take to get downtown?

Chapter Overview

Review the information you learned in this unit.

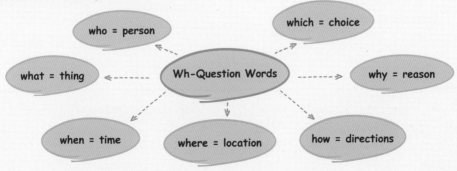

who = person
which = choice
what = thing
Wh-Question Words
why = reason
when = time
where = location
how = directions

Isn't he too busy? (Negative Questions and Tag Questions)

◀)) 21

Conversation | Listen carefully to the negative questions and the tag questions in the conversation.

A Can't we finish this work tomorrow?

B Don't you want to stay for one more hour? Then, we can finish everything.

A David is still here, isn't he? We can get some help from him.

B **Isn't** he too busy? We should leave him alone.

Grammar Focus

① Make negative questions like this:

auxiliary verb + n't + subject	**Aren't** you tired? **Can't** we leave now? **Won't** you try some food?
auxiliary verb + subject + not	**Are** you **not** tired? **Can** we **not** leave now? **Will** you **not** try some food?

Use contractions in conversations and casual speech. Avoid using contractions in formal speech.

② Use negative questions to ask for confirmation of something you believe is true. You can also use negative questions to express surprise that something has not happened yet.

▸ **Didn't** you take out the garbage? (I believe you took out the garbage.)

▸ **Wouldn't** it be fun to take a trip? (I believe it would be fun to take a trip.)

▸ **Have** you **not** finished yet? (I'm surprised you are not finished yet.)

③ Use negative questions to make offers and invitations. These usually begin with **won't you, wouldn't you,** and **why don't you.**

▸ **Won't you** please sit down?

▸ **Wouldn't you** like a drink?

▸ **Why don't you** go with us?

🗨 **Let's check!** Read each sentence and mark O if it is correct and X if it is incorrect.

1 Will not you help me with this?   [   ]   3 Haven't you talked to Sue yet?   [   ]

2 Didn't she bought a new car?   [   ]   4 Is this be not the correct answer?   [   ]

Exercise I

A Complete the sentences with the words in parentheses to make negative questions.

1. _____ you _____ give me some more time, please? (will)

2. _____ we ask for directions to the stadium? (should)

3. _____ you hear me at all? (can)

4. _____ this the house you want to buy? (be)

5. _____ you _____ understand this question? (do)

6. _____ Carol already talk to you? (did)

7. _____ you prefer to take the bus? (would)

directions *(n)* instructions on how to go somewhere

stadium *(n)* an arena where people play sports

B Complete the sentences with the words in the box. Use the words to make negative questions.

do	will	is	were	should	has

1. _____ your name Fred Carter?

2. _____ we take a break for a while?

3. _____ you invite us into your home?

4. _____ you _____ remember her phone number?

5. _____ anyone fixed this problem yet?

6. _____ you _____ talking to Beth yesterday?

break *(n)* a short period of time when you have a rest

Switch It Up!

Read the following answers and write negative questions based on them. Then, ask and answer the questions with your partner.

	Question	Answer
	Aren't you a banker?	No, I'm not a banker.
1		Yes, we should go to bed soon.
2		No, I will not stay a bit longer.
3		Yes, it would be exciting to go camping.
4		No, Ariel did not remember to turn off the lights.
5		Yes, we can watch a movie this evening.

Exercise 11

A Correct the underlined parts.

1 Doesn't Jeff <u>works</u> in this office?

2 Will <u>not</u> you consider our offer?

3 Why you <u>don't</u> visit your parents this weekend?

4 <u>Would not</u> you like to have dinner with us?

5 Are <u>not</u> you the leader of this group?

6 Isn't this <u>be</u> a sugar-free drink?

7 <u>Hasn't</u> the packages been mailed yet?

B Unscramble the words to complete the sentences.

1 anyone / give / help / can't / me / some

2 doesn't / a big city / live / your / in / brother

3 this idea / are / interested / not / you / in

4 some / you / won't / me / money / lend

5 not / ordered / yet / have / any / you / food

6 the problem / us / didn't / about / Janet / tell

7 an email / why / me / you / send / don't

sugar-free *(adj)* having no sugar

mail *(v)* to send something through the post office

90

Grammar Plus⁺

Use tag questions to ask for confirmation of something you believe is true. They mean something like "Is that right?" or "Do you agree?" Form a tag by using the same auxiliary verb used in the sentence in a contraction with **not** and a pronoun. Use a negative tag for a positive question.

▸ You *are* going home soon, **aren't you**?

▸ David *will* call me later, **won't he**?

▸ Margaret *ate* pizza tonight, **didn't she**?

*When there is no auxiliary verb in a sentence, use **do**, **does**, or **did**.

Use a positive tag for a negative question. So do not use the word **not** in the tag.

▸ I *cannot* go on the trip, **can I**?

▸ Travis *hasn't* visited, **has he**?

▸ The game *hasn't* finished, **has it**?

Grammar in Action | Fill in the blanks with the correct tag questions. Then, practice the dialogs with your partner.

1 **A** You can go to the movies with me, _____ ?

  B Sorry, but I'm too busy now. You understand, _____ ?

2 **A** You aren't going out for lunch now, _____ ?

  B I have to stay here in the office. If you're going out, can you get a sandwich for me?

  A Sure. You want a ham and cheese sandwich, _____ ?

3 **A** My report looks all right, _____ ?

  B It has a few problems. You'd like me to go over it, _____ ?

  A I'd love that. Thanks for the offer.

Chapter Overview

Review the information you learned in this unit.

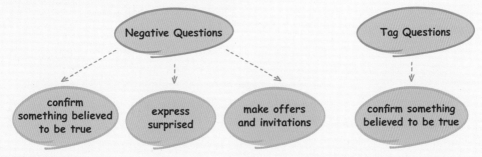

UNIT 21 **91**

Let's go out for some food.

(Suggestions, Imperatives, and Exclamations)

◀)) 22

Conversation | Listen carefully to the suggestions, the imperatives, and the exclamations.

A Wow! What a great TV program that was!

B I agree. I'm hungry now. **Let's go** out for some food.

A Why don't we just cook some food at home instead?

B Sure. Check the fridge to see what food we have.

Grammar Focus

① Make suggestions in English like this:

Let's + verb	"**Let's have** dinner at a restaurant tonight." "I'd love to."
Why don't we + verb?	"**Why don't we see** a movie this weekend?" "Sorry. I can't."
How about + verb -ing?	"**How about taking** a break for a while?" "That's a great idea."
What about + verb -ing?	"**What about buying** that black car?" "I don't have enough money."

② Use **let's** and **let's not** to make suggestions about doing something with another person.

  ▸ **Let's visit** Mark at his workplace today.

  ▸ **Let's buy** a present for Susan.

  ▸ **Let's not go** to the party at the nightclub.

③ Use **why don't we**, **how about**, and **what about** in more formal situations than **let's**.

  ▸ **Why don't we email** Mr. Anderson about these changes?

  ▸ **How about contacting** our supplier now?

  ▸ **What about going** on a trip to London?

④ Use imperatives to give orders, directions, commands, warnings, and requests. In an imperative, the subject is *you*, but do not use *you* in the sentence. Use the infinitive form of the verb without *to*. Make negative infinitives by using **do not + verb**. Make polite requests with imperatives by adding *please* to the sentences.

  ▸ **Be** careful.
  ▸ **Call** me in ten minutes.
  ▸ **Do not let** anyone in the room.

  ▸ *Please* **help** me with this.
  ▸ *Please* **lend** me some money.
  ▸ **Open** the window, *please*.

💬 **Let's check!** Read each sentence and mark O if it is correct and X if it is incorrect.

1 How about cook steak for dinner?   [   ]   **3** Do not give him the information.   [   ]

2 Let's meet at ten in the morning.   [   ]   **4** You pay for this, please.   [   ]

Exercise I

A Complete the sentences with the words in parentheses. Use the correct suggestion with each verb.

1 _____ we _____ the exhibit at the museum? (see)

2 _____ about this problem later. (talk)

3 _____ about _____ the train to Busan? (take)

4 _____ about _____ me a few more minutes to finish? (give)

5 _____ we _____ the presents at the birthday party? (open)

6 _____ this matter with Ms. Woodruff tomorrow. (discuss)

exhibit *(n)* a display

matter *(n)* an issue or problem

B Complete the sentences with the words in the box. Make a positive or negative imperative for each sentence.

pick up	repeat	forget	make	ask	submit

1 _____ so much noise.

2 _____ your friend if he knows the answer.

3 Please _____ that comment one more time.

4 _____ the assignment by the end of the week.

5 _____ the Australian client at the airport, please.

6 _____ to turn off the lights.

comment *(n)* a statement

assignment *(n)* a work project

turn off *(v)* to stop something from operating

Switch It Up!

Read each of the activities below. Then, make suggestions to your partner by using them and see if your partner agrees or turns you down.

going out to eat

1 lending someone some money

2 watching TV at home

3 paying for tickets

4 relaxing at the park

5 camping

6 fixing a computer

7 driving someone to work

A *Let's go out to eat.*

B *I'm sorry, but I already have plans for tonight.*

▶ Go to page 154 to see more responses to suggestions.

Exercise II

A Correct the underlined parts.

1 Please <u>carrying</u> these boxes to the back room.

2 Let's <u>to</u> organize the meeting for the vice president.

organize *(v)* to set up and prepare for something

vice president *(n)* the second-highest person in control of a group, business, etc.

3 <u>What</u> don't we look for a new home in the city?

4 Do not <u>tells</u> anyone about this problem.

5 How about <u>we</u> going for a walk in the morning?

go for a walk *(v)* to go outside and to walk

6 What about <u>wear</u> warm clothes outside?

7 <u>You</u> stop bothering all of these people.

B Match the sentences.

1 Let's go to the amusement park today. [   ]

amusement *(n)* fun

2 How about having dinner soon? [   ]

3 Please show me how to use the software. [   ]

4 How about driving us downtown? [   ]

downtown *(adv)* to the central part of a city

5 Why don't we go dancing tonight? [   ]

6 What about meeting my friends at five? [   ]

7 Do not tell anyone my secret. [   ]

secret *(n)* something others do not know

a. Sure. But my car needs gas.
b. I'll keep my mouth shut.
c. I'd rather stay home.
d. Sorry. I'm not hungry.
e. Six would be better.
f. I'm not good with computers.
g. That sounds like fun.

shut *(v)* to close

Grammar Plus⁺

Use exclamations to express strong emotions, surprise, or shock. Put an exclamation point (!) at the end of an exclamatory sentence. Many exclamatory sentences begin with **What** or **How**.

Do not use too many exclamatory sentences. Using too many makes your writing look bad. In addition, do not use multiple exclamation points at the end of sentence:

Wow!!!! (X)

In addition, do not use both an exclamation point and a question mark together:

What's this!? (X)

▸ **What** a wonderful surprise!

▸ **How** fascinating that story was!

▸ **What** a great answer he gave!

Use an exclamation point after exclamations such as **oops, yahoo, hooray, boohoo, uh-oh, oh, no**, and **boo**.

▸ **Boo**! I scared you.

▸ **Oops**! I dropped the vase and broke it.

▸ **Yahoo**! I just won the lottery.

▸ *Go to page 154 to see more exclamations.*

Grammar in Action | Fill in the blanks with the words you learned above. Then, practice the dialogs with your partner.

1 A _____ ! I have a huge problem. I forgot to pick up the client.

  B _____ ! You'd better call her up and apologize.

2 A _____ ! I have some great news.

  B _____ interesting! What's going on? Tell me about it.

  A I was just accepted to medical school. I'm going to become a doctor.

3 A Look at this. _____ a great game they are playing!

  B Who is winning the game?

  A My favorite team is. _____ ! They just scored another goal.

Chapter Overview

Review the information you learned in this unit.

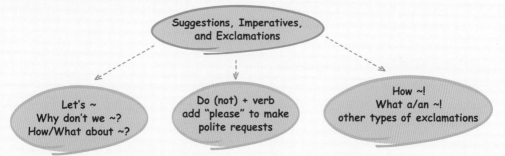

Suggestions, Imperatives, and Exclamations

Let's ~
Why don't we ~?
How/What about ~?

Do (not) + verb
add "please" to make
polite requests

How ~!
What a/an ~!
other types of exclamations

Margaret **said that** you are feeling sick today. (Direct and Indirect Speech)

◀)) 23

Conversation | Listen carefully to the direct and indirect speech in the conversation.

A Margaret **said that** you are feeling sick today.

B That's right. I told my supervisor, "I'm sick and need to go home."

A Then go home now. I'll take care of your work assignments.

Grammar Focus

① **Use direct speech to report the exact words a person says.**

I said, "That's a great idea."

→ Use words like *say, tell, ask, reply,* and *answer* to show you are quoting someone. Direct speech is mostly used in the past tense.

→ Use a comma after those words or before them in a sentence.

→ Use quotation marks (" ") to show the words a person says.

▸ Mr. Jackson told us, **"You shouldn't do that."**

▸ **"What are you doing?"** asked Ms. Holmes.

*When the quoted part comes first in the sentence, words such as *say, tell, ask, reply,* and *answer* can come before or after the subject. However, if the subject is a pronoun, it should come before the verb.

"I'm happy," said Tom. (O)   "I'm happy," Tom said. (O)   "I'm happy," said he. (X)   "I'm happy," he said. (O)

② **Use indirect speech to report something a person said.**

Mary **said that** she wanted to go.

→ Use words such as *say, tell, ask,* and *reply* when using indirect speech. Indirect speech is almost always used in the past tense.

→ In indirect speech, the words are not exact, so do not use quotation marks. In many cases, you should use *that* as well.

▸ The policeman **told** the driver to obey the law.

▸ Mr. Robinson **asked** us to be quiet.

▸ The woman **replied that** she was okay.

③ **Change sentences from direct to indirect speech like this:**

▸ Ronald told me, **"Stop doing that."**

→ Ronald **told me that** I should stop doing that.

▸ Greg asked, **"What is that person doing?"**

→ Greg **asked what** that person was doing.

▸ Lisa replied, **"I'm hungry."**

→ Lisa **replied that** she was hungry.

💬 **Let's check!** Read each sentence and mark O if it is correct and X if it is incorrect.

1 I answered, "No, thank you."   [   ]   **3** The bus driver told us to get off the bus.   [   ]

2 She said that, "This is correct."   [   ]   **4** "I can do that.", he said.   [   ]

Exercise I

A Correct the underlined parts.

1 The manager asked if <u>has anyone</u> a question.

manager *(n)* a person who supervises others

2 She said <u>me</u> that she is taking a trip soon.

3 I told them <u>that</u>, "You're doing it the right way."

4 Mr. Duncan told <u>to</u> his son to do his chores.

5 The customer said, "I'd like to buy this <u>one</u>".

6 He <u>replied</u> "I'm sorry, but I don't have time."

B Make sentences using direct and indirect speech on your own.

I'm taking the bus home. (direct)

He said, "I'm taking the bus home."

1 She was tired. (indirect)

2 Do you have any ice cream? (direct)

3 I don't know where it is. (direct)

4 We would be landing soon. (indirect)

land *(v)* to go to from the sky to the ground

5 There were no more cakes. (indirect)

Switch It Up!

Think about a person you and your partner both know. One person makes positive comments about that person while the other makes negative comments. Then, tell a third person what your partner said by using indirect speech.

A *I like John. He works very hard, and he is intelligent.*

B *I dislike John. He is not polite, and he has bad manners.*

A *B said that he dislikes John. He told me that John is not polite...*

Exercise II

A Read the statements in the box. Then, change them to indirect speech and use them to complete the sentences.

> "You should calm down."   "Please repeat what you said."
> "I want to see a movie with you." "Do you have a question?"
> "Could I borrow your laptop?"

repeat *(v)* to say or do again

1 Kevin looked very nervous. I told him that

   _____.

2 Brenda needed to use a computer. She asked Tim if

   _____.

3 The manager saw Peter raise his hand. He asked Peter if

raise *(v)* to lift or pick up

   _____.

4 I didn't hear Fred's comment. I asked him to

   _____.

5 Zack wanted to go out with Tina. He said that

go out with *(v)* to go on a date with

   _____.

B Change the sentences from direct speech to indirect speech.

1 Brian said to us, "I want to see a movie."

   → _____

2 Patricia asked me, "Where are you going?"

   → _____

3 The teacher replied, "Eric gave a good answer."

   → _____

4 Larry told Jeff, "Don't do that."

   → _____

5 Sandra said to Mary, "You are wrong."

   → _____

6 Mr. Smith asked him, "What's the problem?"

   → _____

7 I replied, "I don't have enough money."

enough *(adj)* sufficient for what one needs

   → _____

Grammar Plus⁺

Use direct speech to give quotations in the present tense and the future tense.

▶ My mother always **tells** me, "Try your best."

▶ When the judge walks in, someone **says**, "All rise."

▶ The boss **will tell** us, "You are not working hard enough."

Use indirect speech to report speech in the present tense and the future tense.

▶ David often **says** that he dislikes spending money.

▶ Julie **will** probably **say** that she doesn't have any time.

▶ Mr. Foster **will tell** us that we did a great job.

Grammar in Action | Fill in the blanks with the words you learned above. Then, practice the dialogs with your partner.

1 A What does your baseball coach usually say to the team?

   B He always says the same thing. He _____, "Let's play hard and win the game."

2 A I have to meet with my manager about a promotion soon.

   B What will he say to you?

   A He _____ probably _____ that I can get a better position next year.

3 A What are you going to tell everyone at the workshop?

   B I _____ them that they should pay close attention.

   A You should also _____ them to read the manual. Then, they can learn faster.

Chapter Overview

Review the information you learned in this unit.

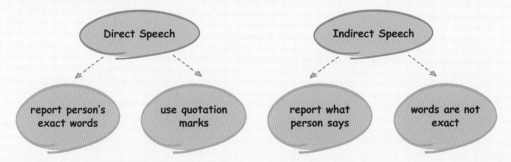

Direct Speech — report person's exact words / use quotation marks

Indirect Speech — report what person says / words are not exact

If you need help, I can do something for you. (Subordinating Conjunctions I)

◀)) 24

Conversation | Listen carefully to the subordinating conjunctions in the conversation.

A I have too much work today.

B **If** you need help, I can do something for you.

A Thanks, Jim. **While** I'm writing this report, can you review the sales figures?

Grammar Focus

① Use subordinating conjunctions to show time and condition:

time	when, while, as soon as	**When** you finish your work, you can eat lunch. She was taking a nap **while** I was watching TV. Please call me **as soon as** you arrive at the café.
condition	if, unless, in case	**If** the phone rings, Sue will answer it. Let's take a taxi **unless** you want to drive. You should bring an umbrella **in case** it rains.

② Subordinating conjunctions combine an independent clause with a dependent clause. The clause with the conjunction is a dependent clause. It cannot stand by itself as a complete sentence.

▸ When I am hungry. (not a complete sentence)

▸ If it's okay with you. (not a complete sentence)

▸ In case nobody is home. (not a complete sentence)

③ Conjunctions used to show time indicate when the action in the main clause took place or will take place.

▸ **When** the game ends, we will go home.

▸ I started studying **as soon as** I heard about the exam.

④ Conjunctions used to show condition indicate rules—or circumstances—that apply to the action in the main clause.

▸ **If** Karen works hard, she will earn a lot of money.

▸ You cannot make dinner **unless** you go shopping first.

Let's check! Read each sentence and mark O if it is correct and X if it is incorrect.

1 When she gets paid, she will buy a new laptop. [　]　**3** As soon as the TV program is finished. 　[　]

2 In case there is something to do. 　　　　　[　]　**4** I will be happy if my boss gives me a raise. [　]

Exercise I

A Circle the correct words to complete the sentences.

1 (When / Unless) the clothes dry, you can put them on.

2 Janet can cut the vegetables (unless / while) I cook the meat.

3 (If / While) we win the game, we will have a big party.

4 You should call the fire department (in case / unless) there is a fire.

5 (If / As soon as) the doorbell rang, Jeff opened the door.

6 (Unless / When) you are too busy, let's have dinner tonight.

7 Peter was cutting the grass (if / while) Chris was working in the garden.

unless *(conj)* except under some circumstances

put on *(v)* to wear, as in clothes

while *(conj)* during

in case *(conj)* if

as soon as *(conj)* when

doorbell *(n)* a chime a person outside rings to ask to be let into a house

B Complete the sentences with the words in the box.

when   unless   if   as soon as   in case   while

1 _____ you apologize, I will be very angry with you.

2 _____ Ms. Davis arrives, please show her to my office.

3 They ate dinner _____ watching a movie on television.

4 The game ended _____ the referee blew his whistle.

5 _____ you have a problem, call Jason for help.

6 We will have the seminar _____ enough people sign up.

referee *(n)* a person who judges a game

blow *(v)* to send air into

whistle *(n)* a device that makes a loud sound when air is blown into it

sign up *(v)* to register

Switch It Up!

Complete the sentences by filling in the blanks with your own ideas. Then, read your sentences together with your partner.

1 When I go home today, _____.

2 If it rains on the weekend, _____.

3 While I was going to work/school yesterday, _____.

4 As soon as the weekend comes, _____.

5 Unless I am too busy tonight, _____.

6 In case my best friend calls, _____.

Exercise 11

A Combine the sentences by using subordinating conjunctions.

1 You go outside at night. You can see many stars. (if)

2 David answered the phone. It rang. (as soon as)

3 Janet was taking a nap. Melissa called her on the phone. (while)

take a nap *(v)* to sleep for a short amount of time

4 We can eat lunch in one hour. You are hungry now. (unless)

in *(prep)* within a certain amount of time

5 We can relax for a while. You need a break. (in case)

6 The game finishes. Let's go for a walk in the park. (when)

B Unscramble the words to complete the sentences.

1 came / Nancy / taking / a visitor / a nap / while / was

2 that book / some money / I / unless / I / from you / cannot / borrow / can / buy

3 would like / some time / if / to meet / you / with you / have / I

4 umbrellas / rains / most / when / carry / it / people

5 John / for them / the items / received / paid / as soon as / he

pay for *(v)* to spend money on something

6 can lend / do not have / some / you / you / in case / I / enough money

Grammar Plus⁺

A subordinating conjunction can be the first word in a sentence or be in the middle of a sentence. When it is the first word in a sentence, use a comma to separate the two clauses. Do not use a comma when the subordinating conjunction is in the middle of a sentence.

- **As soon as** Harry calls, please tell me. / Please tell me **as soon as** Harry calls.
- **If** we make the deal, I will buy dinner. / I will buy dinner **if** we make the deal.
- **When** you finish the book, let me have it. / Let me have the book **when** you finish it.

Conjunctions used to show time are often used first to stress the importance of time. Conjunctions used to show condition often come first in sentences.

- **While** Susan is cleaning the room, Mark will wash the dishes.
- **If** the plane lands by 3:00, we can meet Mr. Reynolds for dinner.

Grammar in Action | Fill in the blanks with the words you learned above. Then, practice the dialogs with your partner.

1 A When are you meeting Mr. Rogers?
   B _____ he finishes his meeting soon, we will meet at 11:00.

2 A Did you finish the report yet?
   B No. I will email it to you _____ I complete it.
   A Please hurry. We are running out of time.

3 A _____ you wait for us, what are you going to do?
   B Nothing. I am just going to sit here.
   A _____ you get bored, you can read this magazine.

Chapter Overview

Review the information you learned in this unit.

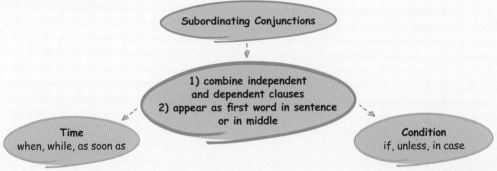

Subordinating Conjunctions

1) combine independent and dependent clauses
2) appear as first word in sentence or in middle

Time
when, while, as soon as

Condition
if, unless, in case

I usually drink coffee **because** I am still sleepy. (Subordinating Conjunctions II)

◀)) 25

Conversation | Listen carefully to the subordinating conjunctions in the conversation.

A When you arrive at the office, what do you do?

B I usually drink coffee **because** I am still sleepy.

A While I'm also sleepy then, I drink tea instead of coffee.

Grammar Focus

① Use subordinating conjunctions to show reason, concession, and contrast:

reason	because
concession	although, though, even though
contrast	while, whereas

Because it is sunny, we can go hiking.

Although I am tired, I can help you.

Though the other team was good, we won.

They went camping **even though** it was cold.

While Jasmine likes beef, Sue prefers chicken.

Kevin is a soldier **whereas** Mark is a banker.

② Conjunctions used to show reason indicate why the activity in the main clause happened.

▸ **Because** I was busy, I did not wash the dishes.

▸ Lisa is happy **because** she won the lottery.

▸ **Because** today is January 1, it is a holiday.

③ Conjunctions used to show concession indicate that an action took place in spite of some type of obstacle.

▸ **Although** there was a traffic jam, I was not late for work.

▸ Marty attended the musical **though** he did not want to.

▸ **Even though** Karen studied, she did not pass the exam.

④ Conjunctions used to show contrast indicate a contrast between two people, places, or things.

▸ **While** Tokyo is a fun city, we prefer Osaka.

▸ Julie loves eating at restaurant **while** Tim likes cooking at home.

💬 **Let's check!** Read each sentence and mark O if it is correct and X if it is incorrect.

1 Because it is late, you can go home now. [   ]   **3** Though he is the boss, you must listen to him. [   ]

2 While we had a great time at the party. [   ]   **4** Although it is late, she is still watching TV. [   ]

Exercise 1

A Circle the correct words to complete the sentences.

1 (Because / Although) the clothes are not dry, you cannot put them on.

2 (If / Although) you are very busy, you are doing good work.

3 (Whereas / Because) Diane works hard, Jacob is lazy.

lazy *(adj)* not wanting to work hard

4 (Though / Because) it is getting dark, the children are still playing outside.

5 Iris dislikes Kevin (if / because) he is frequently rude to her.

frequently *(adv)* often

rude *(adj)* having bad manners

6 (Even though / Whereas) Brenda got up, she was still tired.

get up *(v)* to wake up

B Complete the sentences with the words in the box.

because   whereas   although   while   even though   though

1 _____ they are close, they often hang out together.

hang out *(v)* to spend time with in social situations

2 _____ you apologized, Chrissy is still upset with you.

3 Doug plans to major in English _____ Emily will major in biology.

major *(v)* to study a certain topic at school

biology *(n)* the study of life

4 Somebody broke into the office _____ the door was locked.

break into *(v)* to enter a place by using force

5 _____ Greg received a pay raise, he decided to quit his job.

quit *(v)* to stop doing something

6 _____ Darlene enjoys math, her sister prefers science.

Switch It Up!

Complete the sentences by filling in the blanks with your own ideas. Then, read your sentences together with your partner.

1 Even though I am tired, _____ .

2 Because I feel happy, _____ .

3 Whereas my best friend is kind, _____ .

4 Although I have visited another country before, _____ .

5 While I enjoy Italian food, _____ .

6 Though I do not have much time, _____ .

Exercise II

A Correct the underlined parts.

1 <u>Though</u> you like to look at stars, you should go outside at night.

2 Addison wakes up early <u>while</u> his work starts at 7:30.

3 <u>Because</u> Janet prefers dresses, Alice likes to wear skirts.

4 <u>Whereas</u> I didn't know the answer, I tried to solve the problem.

5 Harry is a good swimmer <u>though</u> he has practiced for many years.

6 <u>Because</u> David plays sports, his brother likes video games.

7 I will lend you some money <u>whereas</u> I cannot afford to.

afford *(v)* to have enough money to pay for something

B Unscramble the words to complete the sentences.

1 Nolan / he / did well / happy / because / was / on the test

....

2 Nancy / to lunch / even though / she / go / was / did not / hungry

....

3 although / a goal / a bad player / scored / Vincent / he / was

score *(v)* to make a goal or to get a point in a game

....

4 Allen / Eric / drives / whereas / a truck / a sports car / drives

....

5 Carol / is getting / stop / because / you / upset / she / should / teasing

tease *(v)* to bother a person by joking around

....

6 Kyle / Andrew / is wearing / a blue shirt / is wearing / a green one / whereas

....

7 enough / the car / I / had / did not / I / though / purchase / money

purchase *(v)* to buy

....

Grammar Plus⁺

Use **though**, **although**, and **even though** to show a contrast. They all have very similar meanings. Use them to describe a situation that currently exists. **Even if**, however, has a different meaning. Use **even if** to discuss something that might happen in the future. It may or may not happen in reality.

▸ **Though** she is sleepy, she will keep working. (She is sleepy. But she will keep working.)
▸ **Even if** she is sleepy, she will keep working. (She might get sleepy later. But she will keep working.)

Use **whenever** to have the meaning of "at any time." Use **wherever** to have the meaning of "at any place." Both words are subordinating conjunctions.

▸ **Whenever** you have time, we can get together.
▸ People recognize the famous movie star **wherever** she is.

Grammar in Action | Fill in the blanks with the words you learned above. Then, practice the dialogs with your partner.

1 **A** Can you afford to take this trip? Isn't it expensive?

   B _____ I have no money, I will go on this trip. I need a vacation.

2 **A** I'd like to meet you _____ you are available.

   B I'm pretty busy these days. _____ I have some free time later today, it won't be for long.

   A That's fine. I just need about ten minutes of your time.

3 **A** _____ the new product is selling well, our stock price is down.

   B That's strange. How can we make it go up?

   A _____ I figure that out, I will let you know.

Chapter Overview

Review the information you learned in this unit.

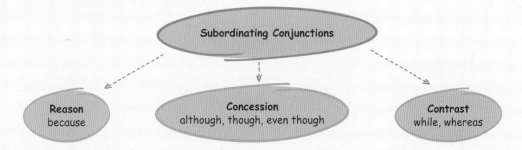

Subordinating Conjunctions

Reason
because

Concession
although, though, even though

Contrast
while, whereas

I'm going to the beach **on** Friday.
(Prepositions of Time)

◀)) 26

Conversation | Listen carefully to the prepositions of time in the conversation.

A What are you doing during the holiday?

B I'm going to the beach **on** Friday. I'll stay there until Sunday.

A That sounds fun. Have a great time.

Grammar Focus

① Use the following prepositions of time:

in	periods of time in a day, months, seasons, years, and longer periods of time, the amount of time needed to do something, and when a future action will happen	He always wakes up **in the morning**. Jane's birthday is **in October**. She completed the job **in three hours**. I will call you **in a while**. They usually take a trip **in summer**.
on	days of the week, dates, special days, and holidays	We will see a movie **on Friday**. He was born **on June 11, 1998**. I will be a ghost **on Halloween**.
at	clock times, mealtimes, specific times of day, festivals, and special events	Let's have the conference **at 3:00**. She goes to bed **at midnight**.
during	when something happens	I plan to travel abroad **during summer vacation.**
by	something must happen before a certain time	Jane must return home **by 11:00 P.M.**
until	a continuous action that stops at a specific time	It rained all week **until Saturday**.

② Use prepositions to connect a noun or noun phrase to another part of the sentence. A noun or noun phrase must always follow a preposition. This is called the object of the preposition.

▸ Alice listened carefully **during** *the presentation*.

▸ People give presents **on** *Christmas*.

▸ We plan to have lunch **at** *noon*.

💬 **Let's check!** Read each sentence and mark O if it is correct and X if it is incorrect.

1 You can stay out during 10:00 P.M. tonight. [   ]   **3** April and May are two months in spring.   [   ]

2 We talked about many things in lunch.   [   ]   **4** We will see a parade on Independence Day. [   ]

Exercise 1

A Circle the correct words to complete the sentences.

1 They will take a flight (in / at / on) Monday.

2 You must arrive at the airport (by / during / at) 8:00 A.M.

3 Lisa practiced the piano (on / until / by) 10:00 at night.

4 Mr. Sanders promised to return the books (in / during / on) a few days.

5 We love to swim (at / during / on) summer.

6 Please call me back (in / by / until) 10 minutes.

B Complete the sentences with the words in the box. Use *in, at, on, during, by,* or *until* in each sentence.

> next Friday   late at night   three weeks
> Thanksgiving Day   7:00 every Tuesday   the winter months

1 The English class starts _____ .

2 They always get together and chat _____ .

3 Susan loves to go skiing _____ .

4 Please submit the science project _____ .   **submit** *(v)* to turn in

5 We plan to visit Australia _____ .

6 Susan said that she will arrive for dinner _____ .

Switch It Up!

Look at the timetable and ask and answer questions with a partner.

	Monday	Tuesday	Wednesday	Thursday	Friday
9:30 ~ 10:20	computer			art	math
10:30 ~ 11:20		math	English	French	
11:30 ~ 12:20		history	biology		
Lunch					
1:30 ~ 2:20	English		physics	biology	history
2:30 ~ 3:20	geography	chemistry			

A *What class do we have at nine thirty on Monday?*

B *We have computer class then.*

Exercise II

A Correct the underlined parts.

1 The new TV program starts <u>until</u> 8:00 P.M.

2 His family will have a picnic <u>until</u> Independence Day.

3 Ms. May will arrive at the office <u>on</u> thirty minutes.

4 We will watch a movie <u>in</u> vacation.

5 My brother must finish cooking dinner <u>in</u> 7:00.

6 The two businessmen met <u>by</u> the meeting.

7 The trip will last from November 18 <u>on</u> December 1.

B Match the sentences.

1 She asks her boss questions   [   ]

2 Valentine's Day takes place   [   ]   **take place** *(v)* to happen; to occur

3 My best friend wants to meet   [   ]

4 The game will start   [   ]

5 The musical will finish   [   ]

6 He read a lot   [   ]

7 The snow fell   [   ]

---

a. by ten at night.
b. during summer vacation.
c. on February 14 every year.
d. during meetings.
e. at the spring festival.
f. until noon.
g. in a few minutes.

noon *(n)* 12:00 in the afternoon

Grammar Plus⁺

Use **in** for the following expressions: **in** *the morning*, **in** *the afternoon*, and **in** *the evening*. But use **at** *night*. In addition, when you add a specific day to these expressions, the preposition changes: **on** *Monday morning*, **on** *Tuesday afternoon*, **on** *Wednesday evening*, and **on** *Thursday night*.

▸ She always drinks coffee **in** *the morning*.   ▸ They watch TV at home **at** *night*.
▸ I have a dinner appointment **on** *Friday evening*. ▸ Let's visit the park **on** *Monday afternoon*.

Do not use any prepositions in front of *this*, *last*, *next*, and *every*.

▸ We are meeting *this weekend*. (NOT on this weekend)
▸ Melanie ate dinner there *last month*. (NOT on last month)
▸ Let's get together *next winter*. (NOT in next winter)
▸ The clock rings *every midnight*. (NOT at every midnight)

Grammar in Action | Fill in the blanks with the words you learned above. Then, practice the dialogs with your partner.

1 **A** Do you have time for dinner _____ Tuesday night?
   B Sorry. I go to the gym _____ Tuesday after work.

2 **A** Did you travel to Indonesia _____ month?
   B Yes. I went there in March and had a great time.
   A I'm going there _____ month in four weeks. Can you tell me about it?

3 **A** I want a meeting with Mr. Carpenter _____ Friday morning.
   B He called today. He is going out of the country _____ Thursday.
   A Okay. Then I want to meet him _____ week.

Chapter Overview

Review the information you learned in this unit.

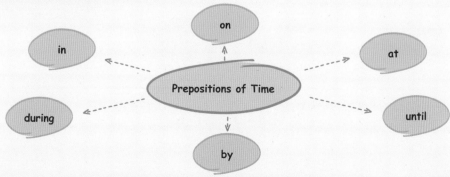

Look **in** the kitchen. (Prepositions of Place)

Conversation | Listen carefully to the prepositions of place in the conversation.

A I can't find my keys. They aren't in the living room.

B Look **in** the kitchen.

A Aha. They were sitting on the table. Thanks.

Grammar Focus

① Use the following prepositions of place:

in	containers, buildings and rooms, geographical areas, towns, cities, and larger places	There is milk **in the carton**. Pierre lives **in France**. The meeting is **in the conference room**. China is a country **in Asia**.
at	specific places, stores, public places, events, and addresses	Let's meet **at the park** tonight. They are eating **at a restaurant** now. We can meet **at 17 Mercer Avenue**.
on	surfaces, streets, and roads	The documents are **on the desk**. Anna lives **on Pine Street**.

*Be careful with street names and addresses. Use **on** with street names but **at** with addresses.
I live **on** First Avenue.   I live **at** 82 First Avenue.

② Use the following prepositions of place to describe specific locations:

in front of

behind / in back of

on

near

above

next to / by / beside

in

between

under

💬 **Let's check!** Read each sentence and mark O if it is correct and X if it is incorrect.

1 The girl is standing in front of the man.   [   ]   **3** The tree is behind of the flowers.   [   ]

2 They will have a drink on the café.   [   ]   **4** Tom is studying hard in his bedroom.   [   ]

Exercise 1

A Circle the correct words to complete the sentences.

1 Mr. Decker is currently (in / at / on) Germany.

2 There is a lot of construction (in / at / on) Orchard Road.

3 There is still some cereal (in / at / on) the box.

4 The festival will be (in / at / on) the town square this weekend.

5 Please visit Ms. Wellman's office (in / at / on) 918 Western Boulevard.

6 The mailman left the envelope (in / at / on) the counter.

7 The book club is meeting (in / at / on) the conference room at the library.

B Complete the sentences with the words in the box.

beside its owner	in front of the TV	between Melanie and Craig
in the lounge	above the skyscrapers	under the rug	on the shelf

1 The bird is flying high _____ .

2 In the classroom, Sebastian always sits _____ .

3 I looked down and found the missing key _____ .

4 In the picture, the dog is sitting _____ .

5 She cannot see the show because the boy is standing

    _____ .

6 You can put the boxes _____ .

7 There are five people waiting _____ .

currently *(adv)* now; at the present time

construction *(n)* the act of building a road, building, bridge, etc.

town square *(n)* a central area in a city

boulevard *(n)* a wide road

mailman *(n)* a person who delivers letters and packages

envelope *(n)* a thin container for letters

conference *(n)* a professional meeting

owner *(n)* a person who possesses something

lounge *(n)* a room where people can relax

skyscraper *(n)* a very tall building

shelf *(n)* a flat surface used to put things on

Switch It Up!

Look at the picture and talk about the location of each item with a partner.

A *Where are the slippers?*

B *They are under the bed.*

Exercise II

A Correct the underlined parts.

1 The telephone is <u>behind of</u> the computer monitor.

2 Several people are meeting <u>on</u> the restaurant tonight.

3 The elevator is <u>in</u> the room and the vending machine.

vending machine *(n)* a machine that sells snacks or drinks

4 Mr. Jackson is on a business trip <u>at</u> Dallas now.

business trip *(n)* travel for the purpose of work

5 Several people are standing <u>near to</u> the celebrity.

celebrity *(n)* a famous person

6 The horse is leaping <u>under</u> the fence.

leap *(v)* to jump, often high or far

7 You can find the company <u>on</u> 777 Lucky Street.

B Match the phrases to make complete sentences.

1 The copy machine is located   [   ]

2 Put the pizza dough   [   ]

3 Turn around and look   [   ]

4 There is a pharmacy   [   ]

pharmacy *(n)* a drugstore

5 The city sponsors free concerts   [   ]

sponsor *(v)* to pay money for an event

6 The boy threw the ball   [   ]

throw *(v)* to use the hand to move something through the air

7 Please do not get too   [   ]

a. above the trees.
b. behind you.
c. between the theater and the restaurant.
d. near the museum exhibits.
e. in the backroom.
f. in the local park.
g. on the pan.

local *(adj)* nearby

Grammar Plus⁺

Use **in** for a movement inside a place, container, or area. Use **in** for something that is a part of another thing, for clothes a person is wearing, and for showing how something is written or expressed.

- I put the boxes **in** *the storage room.*
- Look at that man **in** *the black suit.*
- There are some graphics **in** *her presentation.*
- The dialog in the movie is **in** *Chinese.*

Use **at** for temperatures, speeds, and ages. Use **at** for an activity aimed at a person or thing. Use **on** for movement in the direction of a surface. Use **on** for a body part and for something on a list.

- Water boils **at** *100 degrees Celsius.*
- The airplane flies **at** *the speed of sound.*
- She got a new car **at** *the age of 22.*
- Please do not yell **at** *my friend.*
- The cat jumped **on** *the balcony.*
- That person touched Mary **on** *her arm.*
- We have five items **on** *the agenda.*

Grammar in Action | Fill in the blanks with the words you learned above. Then, practice the dialogs with your partner.

1 A How do you bake a pie?
  B Put it in the oven _____ 200 degrees Celsius for one hour.

2 A Is Tina the woman _____ the blue dress?
  B No, that's Melanie. Tina is the woman walking _____ the carpet.

3 A What is _____ the agenda for the meeting?
  B We'll have a conference call with Mr. Dumont _____ French.
  A _____ French? I studied it _____ the age of 20, but I don't remember much.

Chapter Overview

Review the information you learned in this unit.

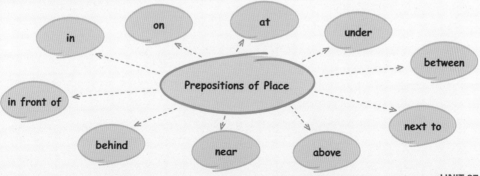

in · on · at · under · between · in front of · Prepositions of Place · behind · near · above · next to

I can't **put off** this project any longer.

(Phrasal Verbs)

🔊 28

Conversation | Listen carefully to the phrasal verbs in the conversation.

A Janet, I need to go over this report with you.

B Do you mind waiting for a while? I'm busy.

A Sorry, but I can't **put off** this project any longer.

Grammar Focus

① A phrasal verb is a verb followed by one or two other words. These words may be prepositions or adverbs. This creates a short phrase. The meaning of a phrasal verb depends on the words following it.

single verb	go	= to move	They **go** to school every day.
verb + adverb	go over	= to review	The students **go over** the material.
verb + preposition	go after	= to follow	He is **going after** his friend.
verb + adverb + preposition	go away from	= to leave	Please **go away from** that building.

② Combine a verb and an adverb to make a phrasal verb. These phrasal verbs can be followed by a direct object or no direct object.

 ▸ Please **turn up** the volume on the radio. (turn up = to make louder)
 ▸ Mr. Harper **put off** the meeting. (put off = to delay)
 ▸ The copy machine **broke down** this morning. (break down = to stop working)

③ Combine a verb and a preposition to make a phrasal verb. All of these phrasal verbs have a direct object.

 ▸ We **talked about** Jeff at the meeting. (talk about = to discuss)
 ▸ The babysitter is **looking after** the children. (look after = to take care of)
 ▸ Please **wait for** me at the train station. (wait for = to stay in one place until something happens)

④ Combine a verb, an adverb, and a preposition to make a phrasal verb. All of these phrasal verbs have a direct object.

 ▸ The car is about to **run out of** gas. (run out of = to use completely)
 ▸ We **look forward to** playing the game. (look forward to = to want to do)
 ▸ I will **get back to** you later. (get back to = to respond to)

💬 **Let's check!** Read each sentence and mark O if it is correct and X if it is incorrect.

1 Let's go over to the information in the book. [   ]   **3** I am waiting for my friend now.   [   ]

2 The mother is after looking her baby.   [   ]   **4** Let's go away from this area now.   [   ]

Exercise 1

A Circle the correct phrasal verbs for the sentences.

1 The teacher will (go over / go after) the test in class.

2 You should not (put in / put off) the decision anymore.

3 It looks like his car (broke down / broke up) this morning.

4 She promised to (get back to / get back on) the client later.

5 We are about to (run out with / run out of) time.

6 He will (turn off / turn up) the music so we can hear it better.

7 Please (look after / look into) my children for a while.

break up *(v)* to divide into separate parts

look into *(v)* to investigate

B Read the sentences and guess the meanings of the underlined phrasal verbs.

1 A thief <u>broke into</u> the store and stole some money.

2 Be sure to <u>look out for</u> mistakes in the paper.

3 The firefighters came and <u>put out</u> the fire.

4 The man <u>ran over</u> a snake in the middle of the road.

5 I believe that Helena <u>comes from</u> Greece.

6 I was surprised when John <u>turned up</u> for the event.

7 After a few years away, he is <u>getting back into</u> his old hobby.

Switch It Up!

Discuss with your partner to match the verbs with the prepositions or adverbs to create phrasal verbs. Then, choose the correct definitions for the words.

1 look •	• out •	• to think of
2 get •	• away •	• to become happier
3 cheer •	• up with •	• to test
4 try •	• for •	• to escape; to go on a vacation
5 drop •	• in •	• to visit someone for a short time
6 come •	• up •	• to try to find
7 cut •	• by •	• to interrupt

Exercise II

Look at the phrasal verbs and their definitions. Then, complete the sentences below by using the correct phrasal verbs.

Phrasal Verbs	Definitions
check in	to get a room at a hotel
catch up with	to get to the same point as another person
give up	to quit
turn down	to reject
pass away	to die
wake up	to get up
find out	to learn
ask out	to invite a person to go on a date
pick out	to choose
pay back	to return some money that was loaned
look up to	to respect or admire
put up with	to tolerate
think about	to consider

1　Harold wants to _____ Teresa on a date.

2　I usually _____ at seven thirty on weekdays.

3　It is hard to _____ his bad manners.

4　Many people _____ the current president.

5　We expect his sick grandfather to _____ sometime soon.

6　The runner is trying to _____ the leader.

7　I need some time to _____ your idea.

8　Guests at the hotel can _____ starting at 1:00 in the afternoon.

9　Please _____ the money you owe Sarah.

10　She went to the store to _____ a new dress.

11　Jeff is going to _____ chance to transfer to London.

12　Anna decided to _____ , so she quit the game.

13　Let's _____ the answer to the question.

current *(adj)* present

owe *(v)* to have to pay money to someone

transfer to *(v)* to move to a different office in a business

Grammar Plus⁺

It is possible to separate some phrasal verbs. These are called separable phrasal verbs. You can do this by putting a noun, noun phrase, or pronoun immediately after the verb. It is possible to separate phrasal verbs with adverbs.

▸ I will **look up** the word in the dictionary. = I will **look** *the word* **up** in the dictionary.

▸ Sarah **broke off** her relationship with Tom. = Sarah **broke** *her relationship with Tom* **off**.

▸ Let's **fill up** the car with gas. = Let's **fill** *the car* **up** with gas.

It is not possible to separate phrasal verbs ending with prepositions. These are called inseparable phrasal verbs. These words must all stay together.

▸ I will **look after** your books. (O)   I will **look** *your books* **after**. (X)

▸ Please **drop by** my house anytime. (O)   Please **drop** *my house* **by** anytime. (X)

▸ Sharon will **run out of** time soon. (O)   Sharon will **run** *time* **out of** soon. (X)

▸ Go to page 155 to see more separable and inseparable phrasal verbs.

Grammar in Action | Fill in the blanks with the words. Then, practice the dialogs with your partner.

1 A Why did you visit Emily last night?

  B She needed someone to _____ . (cheer up)

2 A This problem is too hard. I can't find the answer.

  B Let's try to _____ . (figure out)

  A Okay. We can give it a try.

3 A That movie was so entertaining.

  B Really? I _____ you about that. (disagree with)

  A I'd like to _____ you why you believe that. (hear from)

Chapter Overview

Review the information you learned in this unit.

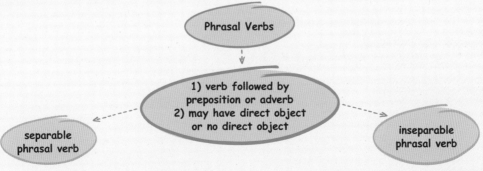

Phrasal Verbs

1) verb followed by preposition or adverb
2) may have direct object or no direct object

separable phrasal verb

inseparable phrasal verb

I **wish** it **were** lunchtime. (Subjunctive Mood)

🔊 29

Conversation | Listen carefully to the verbs in the subjunctive mood in the conversation.

A I'm hungry. I **wish** it **were** lunchtime.

B It's only 10:30. Didn't you eat breakfast?

A I didn't have time because I woke up late.

B If I were you, I'd buy a snack from the vending machine.

Grammar Focus

Use the subjunctive mood to express imaginary situations and conditions that are opposite to fact.

Main Clause	Subordinate Clause
subject + would/could/should + infinitive	if + subject + were + object
	if + subject + were + to-infinitive
	if + subject + did + object
subject + wish	subject + were/did + object

▸ Tom **would cook** dinner for us **if** he **were** here.

▸ I **could help** you out **if** I **were** the manager.

▸ **If** I **were** cold, I **should put** on a jacket.

▸ She **would lend** it to me **if** I **were to ask** for some money.

▸ You **should say** yes **if** Tom **were to offer** you some assistance.

▸ **If** you **were to apply** for the job, you **could get** hired.

▸ You **would gain** weight **if** you **ate** the entire pie.

▸ The police **would catch** him **if** he **stole** the money.

▸ **If** you **won** the lottery, what **would** you **do**?

▸ The students **wish** their grades **were** better.

▸ I **wish** I **had** a car.

▸ Lisa **wishes** she **had** a puppy.

💬 **Let's check!** Read each sentence and mark O if it is correct and X if it is incorrect.

1 If I was you, I would be happy.   [   ] **3** He wishes he knew more people.   [   ]

2 If you drove me to work, I would appreciate it.[   ] **4** If you were to studying, you could learn well. [   ]

Exercise I

A Correct the underlined parts.

1 If I <u>am</u> a bad person, I would try to become good.

> **try** *(v)* to attempt to do something

2 She <u>will</u> answer your question if you asked one.

3 The boss wishes he <u>has</u> some faster workers.

4 If you <u>will read</u> the book, you could tell me about it.

5 Steve could make a lot of money if he <u>works</u> for that company.

6 The woman wishes her car <u>is</u> more expensive.

7 If it rained hard, we <u>canceled</u> the outdoor party.

> **outdoor** *(adj)* relating to being outside

B Complete the sentences with the words in parentheses.

1 If I _____ you, I _____ to Betsy. (be, apologize)

2 If you _____ Jason now, you _____ with him. (call, speak)

3 Where _____ you _____ if you _____ a one-month vacation? (go, have)

4 Everyone _____ they _____ more time to relax. (wish, have)

5 I _____ the job offer if I _____ you. (accept, be)

6 If Chris _____ some money, then he _____ it back. (borrow, pay)

> **pay back** *(v)* to give a person back some money that was loaned

7 The boys _____ the game _____ more interesting. (wish, be)

Switch It Up!

Complete the following sentences by using the subjunctive mood. Then, read the sentences with your partner.

1 If I were rich. . .

2 If I were traveling abroad. . .

3 If I ate too much food. . .

4 If I made my friend angry. . .

5 If I got a job offer in another country. . .

6 If I forgot my cousin's birthday. . .

Exercise II

A Complete the sentences with the words in the box.

| see | have | score | go | know | wash | contact |

1 If Tom were here, he _____ what to do.

2 Peter wishes he _____ the movie with his friends.

3 If our team _____ one more point, we would win the game.

4 I _____ the repairman if my computer were broken.

repairman *(n)* a person whose job is to fix things

5 If Louise used the dishes, then she _____ all of them.

6 I wish I _____ something fun to do this weekend.

7 If you had some free time, where _____ you _____ this weekend?

B Unscramble the words to complete the sentences.

1 Julie / more friends / nicer / would / were / if / have / she

   _____

2 more / you / your skills / you / could / practiced / improve / if

improve *(v)* to get better

   _____

3 Mr. Murphy / for lunch / ate / he / wishes / more

   _____

4 if / more interesting / I / it / finish / the book / were / would

   _____

5 your home / visit / if / Peter / gave / you / him / you / to / would / directions

   _____

6 woman / great / a / she / artist / the / wishes / were

   _____

7 jogging / sunny / would / it / if / were / go / I / today

   _____

Grammar Plus⁺

Use the subjunctive mood to express commands and demands. Use verbs such as **require, insist,** and **demand** followed by **that.** Use the suggestive mood to express suggestions. Use verbs such as **suggest, recommend,** and **propose** followed by **that.** The verb in the **that-**clause can be in the present tense.

▸ Mr. Rogers **demanded that** I **be** on time for work.

▸ The manager **insists that** the employees **act** politely.

▸ We **require that** everyone **wear** a mask.

▸ I **propose that** you **work** more closely with your client.

▸ Jane **recommended that** Eric **be** friendlier to people.

▸ Our CEO **suggests that** we **create** some new products.

> If the verb in the **that-**clause is a **be** verb, use **be.** Do not use *am, is,* or *are.* In addition, do not add *-s, -es,* or *-ies* to the endings of third-person singular verbs when using the subjunctive mood.

Grammar in Action | Correct the underlined parts. Then, practice the dialogs with your partner.

1 A What do you recommend that we <u>done</u>?

  B I propose that we <u>accepts</u> the offer.

2 A Why are you wearing a tie?

  B My boss insists that all employees <u>wearing</u> formal clothes.

  A I hope my boss doesn't suggest <u>to</u> employees <u>does</u> that.

3 A How did your meeting go?

  B Great. I demanded that the company <u>provides</u> better service.

  A You should require that every order <u>arrives</u> on time.

Chapter Overview

Review the information you learned in this unit.

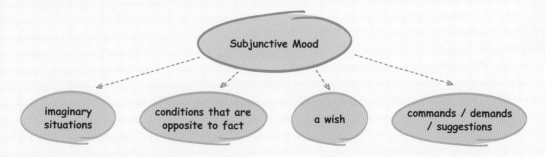

Subjunctive Mood

imaginary situations

conditions that are opposite to fact

a wish

commands / demands / suggestions

I enjoy **swimming** and **hiking**. (Parallel Structure)

🔊 30

Conversation | Listen carefully to the parallel structure in the conversation.

A What do you do in your free time?

B I enjoy **swimming** and **hiking**.

A That sounds fun. I like to watch movies and to bake cookies.

B I like those activities, too.

Grammar Focus

① Use parallel structure when writing about two or more words, phrases, or clauses in the same sentence. When you use a series, you should include nouns with nouns, adjectives with adjectives, verbs with verbs, and adverbs with adverbs. Use conjunctions such as *and* and *or* to create parallel structure.

- ▸ David has a **dog** *and* a **cat**.
- ▸ Carmen is **happy** *and* **pretty**.
- ▸ Peter **plays** baseball *and* **jogs** in the park.
- ▸ Lisa writes **slowly**, **carefully**, *and* **beautifully**.

② Use gerunds with gerunds and infinitives with infinitives. Do not use different forms together in your writing.

Incorrect	Correct
Sara likes **jogging** *and* **to cycle**.	Sara likes **jogging** *and* **cycling**.
I prefer **to take** the bus *or* **driving** my car.	I prefer **to take** the bus *or* **to drive** my car.
Joe's hobbies are **collecting** stamps, **to paint** pictures, *and* **flying** kites.	Joe's hobbies are **collecting** stamps, **painting** pictures, *and* **flying** kites.

③ Use parallel structure when putting two or more clauses together.

Incorrect	Correct
Jeff **went** to the supermarket, **bought** some food, *and* **he cooked** dinner.	Jeff **went** to the supermarket, **bought** some food, *and* **cooked** dinner.
We **will go** on vacation, **travel** to Europe, *and* **we will have** fun.	We **will go** on vacation, **travel** to Europe, *and* **have** fun. OR We **will go** on vacation, **we will travel** to Europe, *and* **we will have** fun.
I have seen that movie, **I have read** that book, *and* **watched** that game.	**I have seen** that movie, **I have read** that book, *and* **I have watched** that game. OR I **have seen** that movie, **read** that book, *and* **watched** that game.

💬 **Let's check!** Read each sentence and mark O if it is correct and X if it is incorrect.

1 We will go skiing or go ice skating in winter. [   ]

2 I want to see a movie or watching a show. [   ]

3 He is having a hamburger, fries, and drinking a coke. [   ]

4 Rose ate dinner, read a book, and went to bed. [   ]

Exercise 1

A Underline the parts of the sentences that show parallel structure.

1 After school, Jack often goes swimming or watches television.

2 There are foxes, deer, and bears in the nearby forest.

3 Please be sure to drive slowly and carefully.

4 It is important to be polite and to have good manners.

5 Susan will call her friend, eat dinner, and read a book after work.

6 The gold necklace is long and shiny.

nearby *(adj)* close

polite *(adj)* behaving properly and with good manners

B Complete the sentences with the words in the box. Use the words in their correct forms.

> fly　return　polite　video games　beautiful　prepare

1 He enjoys playing board games, ＿＿＿＿＿＿＿, and computer games.

2 Playing the piano and ＿＿＿＿＿＿＿ kites are Janet's two hobbies.

3 He can paint pictures steadily and ＿＿＿＿＿＿＿.

4 ＿＿＿＿＿＿＿ and to be honest are two important characteristics.

5 Irene went to the store, bought some items, and ＿＿＿＿＿＿＿ home.

6 We are looking for a person who is considerate, kind, and ＿＿＿＿＿＿＿.

kite *(n)* an object flown in the air

steadily *(adv)* in a regular and even manner

characteristics *(n)* a typical quality of someone or something

considerate *(adj)* kind and helpful

Switch It Up!

Fill in the blanks in the sentences by using parallel structure. Then, read the sentences with your partner.

1 My best friend enjoys ＿＿＿＿＿＿＿ and ＿＿＿＿＿＿＿. (gerunds)

2 I have a cousin who is ＿＿＿＿＿＿＿, ＿＿＿＿＿＿＿, and ＿＿＿＿＿＿＿. (adjectives)

3 It is good to act ＿＿＿＿＿＿＿ or ＿＿＿＿＿＿＿. (adverbs)

4 I always carry ＿＿＿＿＿＿＿, ＿＿＿＿＿＿＿, and ＿＿＿＿＿＿＿ in my bag. (nouns)

Exercise 11

A Read the pairs of sentences and mark the ones that use parallel structure.

1 a. [　] I went in the house, took off my shoes, and then I sat on the couch.

    b. [　] I went in the house, took off my shoes, and sat on the couch.

    couch *(n)* a sofa

2 a. [　] Tom drove his car quickly but safely.

    b. [　] Tom drove his car quickly but safe.

    quickly *(adv)* fast

3 a. [　] Typing fast and answering phones are two requirements for the job.

    b. [　] Typing fast and to answer phones are two requirements for the job.

    requirement *(n)* something that is necessary

4 a. [　] The movie was thrilling, exciting, and mysterious.

    b. [　] The movie was thrilling, exciting, and it was mysterious.

    mysterious *(adj)* relating to something unknown or unexplained

5 a. [　] This letter has some mistakes, incorrect facts, and looks bad, too.

    b. [　] This letter has some mistakes, has incorrect facts, and looks bad, too.

    incorrect *(adj)* wrong

B Correct the underlined parts.

1 Ms. Harper plans <u>go</u> to her hometown and to get some rest.

2 A target can run silently and <u>swift</u>.

    silent *(adj)* quiet
    swift *(adj)* fast

3 Eric is <u>friends</u>, funny, and interesting.

4 We may go to the city by train or <u>plane</u>.

5 I often practice the violin in the morning and <u>night</u>.

6 His favorite activities are driving, <u>to skate</u>, and watching movies.

    activity *(n)* an action

7 Pierre will call a client and <u>talking</u> to her.

Grammar Plus⁺

Use coordinating conjunctions such as *but* and *so* to create parallel structure.

▸ Emily owns a **computer** *but* not **a car**.

▸ The man **felt** hungry, *so* he **ate** dinner.

▸ He sang **loudly** *but* not **clearly**.

Use parallel structure in clauses and phrases by using the same patterns or tenses or by keeping the same voice.

▸ I said **that I felt** sick, **that I needed** a doctor, and **that I should go** to the hospital.

▸ Jane does research **by using** the Internet, **by visiting** the library, and **by speaking** with experts.

▸ The test **was given** at the school, **was taken** by students, and **was graded** by teachers.

Grammar in Action | Fill in the blanks with the words. Then, practice the dialogs with your partner.

1 **A** Where will you apply for a position?

  B I will apply to SMR, Inc., but I _____ to Mercer, Inc. (apply)

2 **A** Why were you late this morning?

  B My alarm clock did not go off, I _____ late, and I _____

    the bus. (wake up, miss)

  A It sounds like you had a bad morning.

3 **A** How do you prefer to get into shape?

  B I do that by running and _____ soccer. (play)

  A As for me, I prefer playing tennis and _____ yoga. (do)

Chapter Overview

Review the information you learned in this unit.

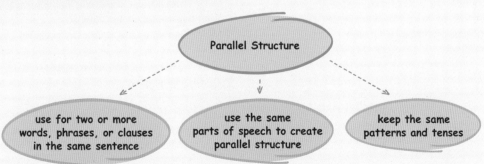

Parallel Structure

use for two or more words, phrases, or clauses in the same sentence

use the same parts of speech to create parallel structure

keep the same patterns and tenses

❗There are often multiple answers to questions requiring readers to write sentences. This answer key only contains the most common answers.

Unit 01

💬 Let's check!

1 O   2 X   3 X   4 O

Exercise I

A

1 don't play	2 travels	3 learn
4 doesn't get	5 bake	6 surfs
7 buy		

B

1 dances	2 begins	3 exercise
4 watch	5 write	6 goes
7 eat		

Exercise II

A

1 Linda and Mark meet for lunch at a restaurant.
2 The cars stop at the red light.
3 I always lock the door at night.
4 Irene does not clean her bedroom on Saturdays.
5 The teacher gives a test every Friday.
6 They read the newspaper on the Internet.
7 We do not live in a big house.
8 I cook dinner with my husband twice a week.

B

1 always	2 gets	3 bakes
4 has	5 opens	6 makes
7 come	8 have	

Grammar in Action

1 arrives	2 rains	3 starts

Unit 02

💬 Let's check!

1 X   2 O   3 X   4 O

Exercise I

A

1 is watering	2 is driving
3 am thinking	4 are not doing
5 are considering	6 are dating
7 are, causing	

B

1 am looking	2 are ordering
3 is buying	4 are asking
5 is getting	6 are watching
7 are riding	

Exercise II

A

1 is	2 swimming
3 not playing	4 asking
5 is working	6 are
7 is talking	

B

1 He is drinking coffee at a café.
2 Mr. Richards and his client are talking about a business opportunity.
3 I'm watching sports on television.
4 Susan is still working at the same company.
5 The leaves are changing colors in fall.
6 Martin is living with his parents.
7 We are eating a large pepperoni pizza for lunch.

Grammar in Action

1 waking, sleeping	2 am staying
3 cooking, putting	

Unit 03

📣 Let's check!

1 X   2 X   3 O   4 O

Exercise I

A

1 walked	2 wrapped	3 drove
4 wrote	5 learned	6 went
7 made		

B

1 ate	2 did not wear
3 were	4 watched
5 did not buy	6 was not

Switch It Up!

1 Christopher Columbus discovered America in the 15th century.
2 Beethoven composed nine symphonies throughout his life.
3 Albert Einstein won the Nobel Prize for Physics in the early 20th century.
4 Shakespeare wrote *Hamlet* in 1601.
5 Genghis Khan founded the Mongol Empire.

Exercise II

A

1 read	2 not	3 brushed
4 ate	5 rode	6 had
7 ~~did~~		

B

1 She studied Spanish with Suzy on Wednesday, October 15.
2 She hosted a dinner party on October 20.
3 She went to the dentist on October 22.
4 She practiced the piano last weekend.
5 She visited her parents on Tuesday.

Grammar in Action

1 lock	2 visited, had
3 dated, made	

Unit 04

📣 Let's check!

1 O   2 X   3 O   4 X

Exercise I

A

1 spent	2 had	3 asked
4 stopped	5 had	6 has

B

1 has jogged
2 had rained
3 have not had
4 had closed
5 has spoken
6 has not replied
7 had won

Switch It Up!

1 Have you met a famous person?
2 Have you done something dangerous?
3 Have you cooked dinner for a lot of people?
4 Have you helped a friend?
5 Have you spoken in front of many people?

Exercise II

A

1 had paid	2 has known
3 have tried	4 had told
5 has heard	6 had sat
7 has grown	

B

1 She has studied French for three years.

2 I did not call her because I had lost her number. / Because I had lost her number, I did not call her.

3 You have forgotten your birthday in the past.

4 The police have not found the thief yet.

5 When she arrived, he had already left the office. / When he arrived, she had already left the office.

6 Because they had brought their passports, they could go to another country. / They could go to another country because they had brought their passports.

7 Mr. Tanner has spoken with Mr. Wayne five times. / Mr. Wayne has spoken with Mr. Tanner five times.

Grammar in Action

1 have just finished

2 had just gotten

3 has just landed

Unit 05

💬 Let's check!

1 O   2 X   3 O   4 X

Exercise I

A

1 are going to attend   2 will buy

3 will be   4 is going to major

5 is going to apply   6 will turn

7 will, do

B

1 will, lend

2 am going to fly

3 will go

4 is not going to watch

5 are going to study

6 will, snow

1 I'll shop at an outlet store tomorrow.

2 I'll have a business dinner on Tuesday.

3 I'm going to take the day off from work this coming Wednesday.

4 I'll go to a barbecue on Thursday.

5 I'm going to relax at home this Friday.

6 I'll see a movie on the weekend.

Exercise II

A

1 ~~am~~   2 deliver

3 drive   4 going to have

5 going to   6 cook

7 is

B

1 e   2 c   3 g   4 a

5 d   6 f   7 b

Grammar in Action

1 is going to rain   2 will have

3 will be

Unit 06

💬 Let's check!

1 X   2 X   3 O   4 O

Exercise I

A

1 could finish

2 can complete

3 May/Could, borrow

4 could be

5 Can, show

6 may work

B

1 may tell
2 Could, wait
3 Can, borrow
4 can bake
5 May/Could, take
6 can meet

Switch It Up!

1 May/Can I borrow your laptop computer? / Could you borrow John's laptop computer?
2 Could you pick up Mr. Smith at the train station? / Can/May I pick up Mr. Smith at the train station?
3 May/Can I turn down the music? / Could you turn down the music?
4 May/Can I cook dinner? / Could you cook dinner?
5 May/Can I help you with your project?
6 May/Can I make a suggestion? / Could you make a suggestion?

Exercise II

A

| 1 I / we | 2 wrap | 3 not |
| 4 not visit | 5 I talk | 6 transfer |

B

1 Can you please repair the motor?
2 May I have your business card?
3 Could you please explain the solution one more time?
4 Can I give you some advice?
5 May I please borrow your sweater?
6 Could you wake me up at 6:30 every day?
7 Can I buy you lunch today?

Grammar in Action

1 can play   2 may learn
3 could/may take

Unit 07

Let's check!

1 O   2 X   3 X   4 O

Exercise I

A

1 must listen / have to listen
2 should see / ought to see
3 must wash / have to wash
4 should vacuum / ought to vacuum
5 should lend / ought to lend
6 must cut / have to cut

B

1 should practice / ought to practice
2 must buy / have to buy
3 should leave / ought to leave
4 must wake up / has to wake up
5 should eat / ought to eat
6 must take / has to take

Switch It Up!

1 You must not ride a bicycle here.
2 You must beware of the dog.
3 You must stay off the grass.
4 You must not park here.
5 You must go right.

Exercise II

A

1 get	2 to	3 ought to go
4 ask	5 do	6 has
7 learn		

B

1 You should finish your chores on time.
2 I have to memorize all of the answers to the questions.
3 He must meet his friend at the theater tonight.
4 Somebody ought to turn off the lights.

5 The girl has to check her schedule every morning.

6 You must remember the way to his house.

7 We should find the missing key now.

Grammar in Action

1 should not go / ought not to go

2 must not steal

3 do not have to attend

Unit 08

💬 **Let's check!**

1 X   2 X   3 O   4 O

Exercise I

A

1 could not solve

2 can make

3 cannot understand

4 could play

5 can pay

6 could not remember

B

1 are not able to complete

2 will be able to visit

3 am not able to meet

4 will be able to suggest

5 is able to read

6 was able to win

Exercise II

A

1 talk   2 will be able   3 couldn't

4 to borrow   5 can   6 attach

7 cannot

B

1 You can install the software on the computer.

2 Mr. Arthur could not consult with the expert this morning.

3 The students are able to establish a new club at the school.

4 She could convince her friends to help her out.

5 I will be able to learn a new language this summer.

6 He was not able to watch the show on television.

7 Lisa cannot find her purse anywhere in her room.

Grammar in Action

1 can   2 am not   3 could

Unit 09

💬 **Let's check!**

1 O   2 X   3 O   4 X

Exercise I

A

1 was disappointed

2 is cleaned

3 were given

4 was built

5 am surprised

6 was directed

7 was invented

B

1 was repaired

2 are taught

3 was offered

4 were trained

5 is considered

6 was rewarded

7 are pleased

1 b 　　2 f 　　3 d 　　4 a
5 e 　　6 c 　　7 g

Exercise II

A

1 is 　　　2 changed 　　3 enjoyed
4 were 　　5 cooked 　　6 cut
7 accepted

B

1 The house was made by the builders.
2 The solution to the problem is explained by Mr. Murphy.
3 My bedroom is cleaned by my mother.
4 The students are criticized by the teacher.
5 Books were placed on the shelves by the librarian.
6 Pies are baked in the oven by the chef.
7 Everyone was saved from the fire by the firefighters.

Grammar in Action

1 to be instructed
2 to be given
3 being promoted, being given

Unit 10

Let's check!

1 X 　　2 X 　　3 O 　　4 O

Exercise I

A

1 to drive 　　2 to solve 　　3 to wear
4 to eat 　　　5 to reserve 　　6 to lose

B

1 to 　　　　2 try 　　3 paint
4 to protect 　5 to take 　6 hear

7 find

John loves to watch movies. But he hates to visit coffee shops. Susan likes to drive cars and doesn't like to wake up early. Kevin likes to go scuba diving, but he doesn't like to stay late at work. Helen loves to jog at the park. But she hates to wait a long time.

Exercise II

A

1 c 　　　2 e 　　3 b
4 d 　　　5 a 　　6 f

B

1 It is boring to stay home on the weekend.
2 Lily wants to buy a new smartphone soon.
3 Mr. Dawson came to do some work for a project.
4 It is hard to argue with some people.
5 I called to ask about our homework.
6 We visited the hospital to see our sick friend.

Grammar in Action

1 enough, to answer
2 who to travel
3 too, to eat, where to go

Unit 11

Let's check!

1 X 　　2 O 　　3 O 　　4 X

Exercise I

A

1 saving 　　2 keeping 　　3 stopping
4 making 　　5 playing 　　6 lying
7 imagining 　8 running 　　9 looking
10 taking 　　11 quitting 　12 dying

B

1 Simon resisted saying anything bad to his friend.
2 Reading books is his favorite free-time activity. / His favorite free-time activity is reading books.
3 The policeman's best skill is catching criminals. / Catching criminals is the policeman's best skill.
4 Trusting your friends is important.
5 Rachel delayed answering the question for ten minutes.
6 One major problem is texting from the driver's seat. / Texting from the driver's seat is one major problem.
7 Dr. White recommends eating healthy food every day.

Switch It Up!

1 She loves <u>talking</u> to her friends on the phone.
그녀는 친구들과 전화로 이야기하는 것을 좋아한다.
2 <u>Following</u> the rules is important to do.
규칙을 따르는 것은 중요하다.
3 June's hobby is <u>watching</u> old movies.
June의 취미는 옛날 영화를 보는 것이다.
4 I remember <u>meeting</u> my cousin last year.
나는 작년에 나의 사촌을 만났던 것을 기억한다.
5 <u>Buying</u> jewelry can be very expensive.
보석을 사는 것은 돈이 많이 들 수 있다.
6 She tries <u>exercising</u> after work every evening.
그녀는 매일 밤 퇴근 후에 운동을 한다.
7 What he remembers is <u>locking</u> the door.
그가 기억해낸 것은 문을 잠갔던 것이다.

Exercise II

A

| 1 working | 2 Becoming | 3 asking |
| 4 getting | 5 opening | 6 Pleasing |

B

| 1 hitting | 2 seeing | 3 taking |
| 4 giving | 5 Finishing | 6 paying |

| 7 cleaning | 8 doing | 9 working |
| 10 Raising | 11 asking | |

Grammar in Action

| 1 going | 2 using | 3 cleaning |

Unit **12**

Let's check!

| 1 X | 2 O | 3 O | 4 X |

Exercise I

A

1 to try	2 taking	3 owning
4 to celebrate	5 making	6 to write
7 cleaning		

B

1 spending	2 raining / to rain
3 to play	4 to contact
5 to hear	6 to arrive
7 accepting	

Exercise II

A

1 having	2 tell
3 to receive	4 writing / to write
5 to provide	6 winning
7 talking	

B

1 Jeff denied forgetting to pay for the items.
2 Roberta hates to wake up early in the morning.
3 You need to manage your team better.
4 Martha enjoys relaxing at the beach during summer.
5 We agreed to go on a picnic this Saturday.
6 You can continue reading the book after dinner.

7 I stopped to draw a picture of the beautiful landscape.

Grammar in Action
1 watching, to go   2 waking up
3 write, to do

Unit 13

💬 Let's check!
1 X   2 O   3 X   4 O

Exercise I

A
1 That man painting is my good friend.
2 Firefighters hurried to the burning house.
3 Sam put the trapped animal in a cage.
4 The disappointed girl got a poor grade.
5 I heard the telephone ringing.
6 Wilma likes to read printed books instead of e-books.
7 The eating dog is very hungry.

B
1 shining   2 Blooming   3 ringing
4 restricted   5 marching   6 precooked
7 annoyed

Switch It Up!
1 The movie is terrifying.
2 The woman is surprised.
3 The students are bored.
4 The rollercoaster is thrilling.
5 The book is interesting.

Exercise II

A
1 growing   2 Processed   3 smiling
4 flying   5 broken   6 sleeping
7 lost

B
1 She lives in the well-built house.
2 The moving train is going fast.
3 They are members of the winning team.
4 I am friends with the laughing boy.
5 I know the respected man in the community.
6 Karen has a broken vase.
7 Mr. Anderson has an office in the renovated building.

Grammar in Action
1 made   2 Driving
3 rising, Surprised

Unit 14

💬 Let's check!
1 O   2 X   3 X   4 O

Exercise I

A
1 O   2 S   3 S
4 O   5 S

B
1 mine   2 their   3 her, hers
4 Our   5 yours

C
1 yourself   2 ourselves   3 herself
4 themselves   5 himself

Switch It Up!
1 Mr. Jacobs talked to them today.
2 She is sitting by herself on a bench.
3 They are taking a training course now.
4 We are walking to the pharmacy.
5 Somebody is talking to him on the phone.
6 Please ask her for some advice.

Exercise II

A

1 me	2 himself	3 her
4 his	5 themselves	6 hers
7 We		

B

1 b	2 c	3 a
4 d	5 a	6 a
7 a		

Grammar in Action

1 It, It, to meet   2 to play, it, It

3 It, to learn, It

Unit 15

📢 Let's check!

1 X   2 O   3 X   4 O

Exercise I

A

1 ø	2 the	3 ø
4 a	5 a	6 The
7 an		

B

1 pollution, is	2 are, lions
3 Gasoline, is	4 people, are
5 Travel, has	6 Rice, tastes
7 dogs, live	

Switch It Up!

1	U	9	U	17	C
2	C	10	C	18	U
3	C	11	U	19	C
4	U	12	C	20	U
5	C	13	C	21	U
6	U	14	C	22	C
7	C	15	U	23	U
8	U	16	U	24	C

Exercise II

1 ~~the~~	2 air
3 salt	4 ~~The~~
5 oranges	6 milk
7 horses	8 ~~The~~
9 pencil	10 the moon
11 equipment	12 the swimming pool
13 ~~a~~	14 luggage
15 ~~a~~	16 sugar
17 a coin	18 ~~the~~

Grammar in Action

1 There, some

2 some, much, some

3 some, any, a few, some

Unit 16

📢 Let's check!

1 O   2 X   3 O   4 X

Exercise I

A

1 heavy	2 slow	3 well
4 angrily	5 usually	6 bad
7 kind		

B

1 boring	2 nice	3 really
4 happily	5 well	6 swift
7 seriously		

Exercise II

A

1 fairly	2 fast	3 really
4 fun	5 slowly	6 high
7 long		

B

1 beautiful   2 hard   3 happily
4 intelligent   5 difficult   6 slowly
7 widely   8 serious

Grammar in Action

1 lonely   2 silly, very   3 lovely, very

Unit 17

💬 Let's check!

1 X   2 O   3 X   4 O

Exercise I

A

1 farther   2 more expensive
3 the tallest   4 better
5 The fastest   6 the largest
7 the most famous

B

1 cleaner   2 faster
3 the hottest   4 the most handsome
5 older   6 more intelligent
7 the heaviest

Switch It Up!

1 The first tree is taller than the second one.
   The third tree is taller than all of the trees.
2 The yellow sock is longer than the red and
   white sock.
   The purple sock is longer than the pink sock.
3 The bull is more dangerous than the sheep.
   The lion is more dangerous than the horse.

Exercise II

A

1 faster   2 the most expensive
3 the wettest   4 politer

---

5 the most beautiful   6 happier
7 the nicest

B

1 cloudier   2 most difficult
3 colder   4 cutest
5 hairier   6 than
7 louder   8 handsome
9 funnier

Grammar in Action

1 as, as, less
2 less, not, as, as, the least
3 as, as, less, not as

Unit 18

💬 Let's check!

1 O   2 X   3 O   4 X

Exercise I

A

1 who   2 which is
3 who / that   4 which
5 which / that   6 who(m) / that
7 which

B

1 who/that works at that company
2 which/that breaks down very often
3 which/that is worth a lot of money
4 who/that cooked your dinner
5 who(m)/that we all knew
6 which/that was really fun

Switch It Up!

1 My best friend is the person whom I always
   talk to.
2 2019 was the year that I got a great job.
3 I remember the trip which I took to Africa.

4 I love food that tastes spicy.

5 I like people who are friendly.

Exercise II

A

1 I love this song, which is called *Home Again*.

2 The man has a car that can go fast.

3 The bus driver, who is an old man, is smiling.

4 You met Ms. Johnson, whom you are related to.

5 The calculator that I bought is broken.

6 She recalls the man who saved her life.

7 I spent all of the money which I earned.

B

1 We remember the game that was exciting.

2 I love novels, which are my favorite books.

3 The dog which is running is a Shi-tzu.

4 Mr. Hampton, whom we respect, is taking a trip.

5 My sister, who is a nurse, works at a hospital.

6 I have an idea that should work well.

7 Many children play soccer, which is a sport. / Soccer, which many children play, is a sport.

Grammar in Action

1 whose

2 whomever, whoever

3 whoever, whose

Unit 19

🗨 Let's check!

1 X   **2** O   **3** X   **4** O

Exercise I

A

1 why   **2** how   **3** where

4 why   **5** when   **6** why

7 where

B

1 where   **2** the time when

3 why   **4** how

5 when   **6** where

7 when

Switch It Up!

1 I want you to explain how to solve the problem.

2 December is the month when people celebrate Christmas.

3 This restaurant is the place where I met my wife.

4 I remember the reason why I do not like that person.

Exercise II

A

1 a   **2** c   **3** b   **4** d

5 g   **6** e   **7** f

B

1 We are going to the theater where the movie is playing.

2 Please state the time when the game starts.

3 She often asks us how we are going home.

4 The hotel where we stayed is expensive.

5 It is in summer when there is a lot of rain.

6 I remember the reason why I failed the test.

7 The beach where Sue lives near is popular with people.

Grammar in Action

1 at/in which   **2** for which, at which

3 in which, for which

Unit 20

1 O   2 X   3 O   4 X

Exercise I

A

1 is   2 does, work
3 do, attend   4 are, flying
5 does, want   6 is watching
7 do, arrive

B

1 How   2 What   3 Where
4 Who   5 Which   6 Why
7 When

Switch It Up!

1 What is your favorite food?
2 Who is your best friend?
3 Where do you live?
4 When do you go to bed?
5 Why does he study hard?
6 How does Mr. Chen like English?
7 Which do you prefer, sports or movies?

Exercise II

A

1 What do they   2 Who
3 were   4 dislike
5 Which does   6 go
7 does

B

1 e   2 f   3 a   4 c
5 d   6 g   7 b

Grammar in Action

1 What   2 How much   3 What

Unit 21

Let's check!

1 X   2 X   3 O   4 X

Exercise I

A

1 Will, not   2 Shouldn't   3 Can't
4 Isn't   5 Do, not   6 Didn't
7 Wouldn't

B

1 Isn't
2 Won't / Shouldn't
3 Won't / Shouldn't
4 Do, not
5 Hasn't
6 Won't / Shouldn't
7 Were, not

Switch It Up!

1 Shouldn't we go to bed soon?
2 Won't you stay a bit longer?
3 Wouldn't it be exciting to go camping?
4 Didn't Ariel remember to turn off the lights?
5 Can't we watch a movie this evening?

Exercise II

A

1 work
2 Will you not consider our offer?
3 Why don't you visit your parents this weekend?
4 Wouldn't
5 Are you not the leader of this group?
6 ~~be~~
7 Haven't

B

1 Can't anyone give me some help?

2 Doesn't your brother live in a big city?

3 Are you not interested in this idea?

4 Won't you lend me some money?

5 Have you not ordered any food yet?

6 Didn't Janet tell us about the problem?

7 Why don't you send me an email?

Grammar in Action

1 can't you, don't you

2 are you, don't you

3 doesn't it, wouldn't you

Unit 22

Let's check!

1 X   2 O   3 O   4 X

Exercise I

A

1 Why don't, see

2 Let's talk

3 How/What, taking

4 How/What, giving

5 Why don't, open

6 Let's discuss

B

1 Don't make   2 Ask

3 repeat   4 Submit

5 Pick up   6 Don't forget

Switch It Up!

1 Why don't you lend her some money?

2 Let's watch TV at home.

3 How about paying for tickets?

4 Why don't we relax at the park?

5 How about camping?

6 What about fixing a computer?

7 Let's drive them to work.

Exercise II

A

1 carry   2 to   3 Why

4 tell   5 we   6 wearing

7 You

B

1 g   2 d   3 f   4 a

5 c   6 e   7 b

Grammar in Action

1 Uh-oh, Oh, no   2 Yahoo, How

3 What, Hooray

Unit 23

Let's check!

1 O   2 X   3 O   4 X

Exercise I

A

1 anyone has   2 me   3 that

4 to   5 one."   6 replied,

B

1 I said that she was tired.

2 You asked, "Do you have any ice cream?"

3 She told me, "I don't know where it is."

4 The pilot said that we would be landing soon.

5 He said there were no more cakes.

Exercise II

A

1 he should calm down

2 she could borrow his laptop

3 he had a question

4 repeat what he said

5 he wanted to see a movie with her

B

1 Brian said that he wanted to see a movie.

2 Patricia asked me where I was going.

3 The teacher replied that Eric gave a good answer.

4 Larry told Jeff not to do that.

5 Sandra told Mary that she was wrong.

6 Mr. Smith asked him what the problem was.

7 I replied that I didn't have enough money.

Grammar in Action

1 says   2 will, say   3 will tell, tell

Unit 24

💬 Let's check!

1 O   2 X   3 X   4 O

Exercise I

A

1 When   2 while   3 If

4 in case   5 As soon as   6 Unless

7 while

B

1 Unless   2 When   3 while

4 as soon as   5 In case / If   6 if

Switch It Up!

1 When I go home today, I will check my email.

2 If it rains on the weekend, I will stay home.

3 While I was going to work yesterday, I saw my best friend on the bus.

4 As soon as the weekend comes, my family will go to the park.

5 Unless I am too busy tonight, I will work on the project.

6 In case my best friend calls, I will apologize to him.

Exercise II

A

1 If you go outside at night, you can see many stars.

2 David answered the phone as soon as it rang.

3 While Janet was taking a nap, Melissa called her on the phone.

4 We can eat lunch in one hour unless you are hungry now.

5 We can relax for a while in case you need a break.

6 When the game finishes, let's go for a walk in the park.

B

1 A visitor came while Nancy was taking a nap.

2 Unless I can borrow some money from you, I cannot buy that book.

3 If you have some time, I would like to meet with you.

4 When it rains, most people carry umbrellas.

5 John received the items as soon as he paid for them.

6 In case you do not have enough money, I can lend you some.

Grammar in Action

1 If   2 as soon as   3 While, If

Unit 25

💬 Let's check!

1 O   2 X   3 X   4 O

Exercise I

A

1 Because   2 Although   3 Whereas

4 Though   5 because   6 Even though

B

1 Because

2 Though / Although / Even though

3 whereas / while

4 though / although / even though

5 Though / Although / Even though

6 Whereas / While

Switch It Up!

1 Even though I am tired, I will finish my homework.

2 Because I feel happy, I cannot stop smiling.

3 Whereas my best friend is kind, my brother is not very nice.

4 Although I have visited another country before, I prefer to take trips in my own country.

5 While I enjoy Italian food, I am eating Spanish food tonight.

6 Though I do not have much time, I will help you with your work.

Exercise II

A

1 Because

2 because

3 Whereas / While

4 Though / Although / Even though

5 because

6 Whereas / While

7 though / although / even though

B

1 Because Nolan did well on the test, he was happy.

2 Even though Nancy was hungry, she did not go to lunch.

3 Although Vincent was a bad player, he scored a goal.

4 Eric drives a sports car whereas Allen drives a truck. / Allen drives a sports car whereas Eric drives a truck.

5 You should stop teasing Carol because she is getting upset.

6 Kyle is wearing a blue shirt whereas Andrew is wearing a green one. / Andrew is wearing a blue shirt whereas Kyle is wearing a green one.

7 Though I had enough money, I did not purchase the car.

Grammar in Action

1 Even if

2 whenever, Even if

3 Even though, Whenever

Unit 26

Let's check!

1 X   2 X   3 O   4 O

Exercise I

A

1 on   2 by   3 until

4 in   5 during   6 in

B

1 at 7:00 every Tuesday

2 until late at night

3 during the winter months

4 by next Friday

5 in three weeks

6 on Thanksgiving Day

Exercise II

A

1 at   2 on   3 in

4 during   5 by   6 during / at

7 until

B

1 d   2 c   3 e   4 g

5 a   6 b   7 f

Grammar in Action

1 on, every   2 last, next

3 on, this, next

Unit 27

💬 Let's check!

1 O   2 X   3 X   4 O

Exercise I

A

1 in   2 on   3 in

4 at   5 at   6 on

7 in

B

1 above the skyscrapers

2 between Melanie and Craig

3 under the rug

4 beside its owner

5 in front of the TV

6 on the shelf

7 in the lounge

Exercise II

A

1 behind   2 at   3 between

4 in   5 near   6 above

7 at

B

1 e   2 g   3 b   4 c

5 f   6 a   7 d

Grammar in Action

1 at   2 in, on   3 on, in, In, at

Unit 28

💬 Let's check!

1 X   2 X   3 O   4 O

Exercise I

A

1 go over   2 put off   3 broke down

4 get back to   5 run out of   6 turn up

7 look after

B

1 break into: to force entry into a place

2 look out for: to check for

3 put out: to extinguish

4 run over: to drive on top of something

5 come from: to originate from

6 turn up: to appear

7 get back into: to start doing something again

Switch It Up!

1 look for: to try to find

2 get away: to escape; to go on a vacation

3 cheer up: to become happier

4 try out: to test

5 drop by: to visit someone for a short time

6 come up with: to think of

7 cut in: to interrupt

Exercise II

1 ask out   2 wake up

3 put up with   4 look up to

5 pass away   6 catch up with

7 think about   8 check in

9 pay back   10 pick out

11 turn down   12 give up

13 find out

Grammar in Action

1 cheer her up
2 figure it out
3 disagree with, hear from

Unit 29

🗨 Let's check!

1 X   2 O   3 O   4 X

Exercise I

A

1 were   2 would   3 had
4 read   5 worked   6 were
7 would cancel

B

1 were, would apologize
2 called, could speak
3 would, go, had
4 wishes, had
5 would accept, were
6 borrowed, should pay
7 wish, were

Switch It Up!

1 If I were rich, I would give some money to my parents.
2 If I were traveling abroad, I would have a great time.
3 If I ate too much food, I would exercise the next day.
4 If I made my friend angry, I would apologize to him.
5 If I got a job offer in another country, I would turn it down.
6 If I forgot my cousin's birthday, I would send her something nice.

Exercise II

A

1 would know   2 saw
3 scored   4 would contact
5 should wash   6 had
7 would, go

B

1 If Julie were nicer, she would have more friends.
2 You could improve your skills if you practiced more.
3 Mr. Murphy wishes he ate more for lunch.
4 If the book were more interesting, I would finish it.
5 Peter would visit you if you gave him directions to your home.
6 The woman wishes she were a great artist.
7 If it were sunny today, I would go jogging.

Grammar in Action

1 do, accept   2 wear, that, do
3 provide, arrive

Unit 30

🗨 Let's check!

1 O   2 X   3 X   4 O

Exercise I

A

1 After school, Jack often <u>goes swimming</u> or <u>watches television</u>.
2 There are <u>foxes</u>, <u>deer</u>, and <u>bears</u> in the nearby forest.
3 Please be sure to drive <u>slowly</u> and <u>carefully</u>.
4 It is important <u>to be polite</u> and <u>to have good manners</u>.
5 Susan will <u>call her friend</u>, <u>eat dinner</u>, and <u>read a book</u> after work.

6 The gold necklace is <u>long</u> and <u>shiny</u>.

B

1 video games   2 flying

3 beautifully   4 To prepare

5 returned   6 polite

Switch It Up!

1 swimming, talking to her friends

2 young, athletic, handsome

3 politely, respectfully

4 pencils, a notepad, a laptop computer

Exercise II

A

1 b   2 a   3 a   4 a

5 b

B

1 to go   2 swiftly   3 friendly

4 by plane   5 at night   6 skating

7 will talk

Grammar in Action

1 will not apply   2 woke up, missed

3 by playing, doing

Vocabulary Index

foreign
private
protect
joke
contact
deliveryman
drop off
argue

Unit **11**
lie
resist
catch
trust
delay
major
involve
goal
raise
reward
discuss
please
raise
attention
report
common
assistance

Unit **12**
deny
countryside
noise
suddenly
expect
destination
offer
argument
employee
receive
bother
provide
lottery

all the time
manage
go on a picnic
continue
draw
landscape

Unit **13**
burning
instead of
bloom
belong to
restrict
march
process
grow
nutrient
object
crib
well-built
respect
vase
renovate

Unit **14**
look for
vehicle
burden
mortgage
broken
hometown
help oneself
bring

Unit **15**
wallet
pollution
run
pour
be located
astronaut

equipment
pack
luggage

Unit **16**
businessman
customer
early
arrest
jail
laugh
agree
make a mistake
take a while
finish
serious
in public
practice

Unit **17**
far
famous
entire
regular
town
manners
cloudy
own
hairy
loud
classical

Unit **18**
leather
cost
prefer
break down
often
chef
recognize
related

calculator
recall
earn
take a trip
work

Unit 19

reason
move
water cycle
celebrate
used to
mention
field
scary
abroad
state
ask
stay
fail
near

Unit 20

attend
invite
upset
easily
depart
dislike
correct
broken
yet

Unit 21

directions
stadium
break
sugar-free
mail

Unit 22

exhibit
matter
comment
assignment
turn off
organize
vice president
go for a walk
amusement
downtown
secret
shut

Unit 23

manager
land
repeat
raise
go out with
enough

Unit 24

unless
put on
while
in case
as soon as
doorbell
referee
blow
whistle
sign up
take a nap
in
pay for

Unit 25

lazy
frequently
rude

get up
hang out
major
biology
break into
quit
afford
score
tease
purchase

Unit 26

submit
take place
noon

Unit 27

currently
construction
town square
boulevard
mailman
envelope
conference
owner
lounge
skyscraper
shelf
vending machine
business trip
celebrity
leap
pharmacy
sponsor
throw
local

Unit 28

break up
look into
current

own
transfer to

Unit **29**
try
outdoor
pay back
repairman
improve

Unit **30**
nearby
polite
kite
steadily
characteristics
considerate
couch
quickly
requirement
mysterious
incorrect
silent
swift
activity

Unit 03
Irregular Verbs

Based Form	Simple Past	Past Participle
awake	awoke	awoken
be	was, were	been
bear	bore	born
beat	beat	beat
become	became	become
begin	began	begun
bet	bet	bet
bite	bit	bitten
bleed	bled	bled
blow	blew	blown
break	broke	broken
breed	bred	bred
bring	brought	brought
broadcast	broadcast	broadcast
build	built	built
burn	burned / burnt	burned / burnt
buy	bought	bought
cast	cast	cast
catch	caught	caught
choose	chose	chosen
come	came	come
cost	cost	cost
creep	crept	crept
cut	cut	cut
deal	dealt	dealt
dig	dug	dug
dive	dived / dove	dived
do	did	done
draw	drew	drawn
dream	dreamed / dreamt	dreamed / dreamt
drive	drove	driven
drink	drank	drunk
eat	ate	eaten
fall	fell	fallen
feed	fed	fed
feel	felt	felt
fight	fought	fought
find	found	found
fit	fit	fit
fly	flew	flown
forbid	forbade	forbidden
forget	forgot	forgotten
forgive	forgave	forgiven
freeze	froze	frozen
get	got	gotten
give	gave	given
go	went	gone
grind	ground	ground
grow	grew	grown
hang	hung	hung
hear	heard	heard
hide	hid	hidden
hit	hit	hit
hold	held	held
hurt	hurt	hurt
keep	kept	kept
knit	knit	knit
know	knew	know
lay	laid	laid
lead	led	led
leap	leaped / leapt	leaped / leapt
learn	learned / learnt	learned / learnt
leave	left	left
lend	lent	lent
let	let	let
lie	lay	lain
light	lighted / lit	lighted / lit
lose	lost	lost
make	made	made
mean	meant	meant
meet	met	met
mistake	mistook	mistaken
overcome	overcame	overcome
pay	paid	paid
plead	pleaded / pled	pleaded / pled
prove	proved	proved / proven
put	put	put
quit	quit	quit
read	read	read
ride	rode	ridden
ring	rang	rung
rise	rose	risen
run	ran	run
saw	sawed	sawed / sawn
say	said	said
see	saw	seen
seek	sought	sought
sell	sold	sold

send	sent	sent
set	set	set
shake	shook	shaken
shave	shaved	shaved / shaven
shed	shed	shed
shine	shone	shone
shoot	shot	shot
show	showed	showed / shown
shrink	shrank	shrunk
shut	shut	shut
sing	sang	sung
sink	sank	sunk
sit	sat	sat
sleep	slept	slept
slide	slid	slid
speak	spoke	spoken
speed	sped	sped
spend	spent	spent
spill	spilled / spilt	spilled / spilt
spin	spun	spun
spit	spit / spat	spit
split	split	split
spread	spread	spread
stand	stood	stood
steal	stole	stolen
stick	stuck	stuck
sting	stung	stung
stink	stank	stunk
strike	struck	struck
swear	swore	sworn
sweep	swept	swept
swell	swelled	swelled / swollen
swim	swam	swum
swing	swung	swung
take	took	taken
teach	taught	taught
tear	tore	torn
tell	told	told
think	thought	thought
thrive	thrived	thrived
throw	threw	thrown
understand	understood	understood
upset	upset	upset
wake	woke	woken
wear	wore	worn

weave	weaved / wove	weaved / woven
wind	wound	wound
win	won	won
withstand	withstood	withstood
write	wrote	written

Unit 12
Verbs Followed by Gerunds and To-Infinitives

Gerunds	To-Infinitives	Both	Both (Difference in Meanings)
admit	afford	begin	forget
anticipate	agree	cannot bear	go on
appreciate	appear	cannot stand	mean
avoid	arrange	continue	need
cannot help	care	hate	regret
cannot see	claim	intend	remember
complete	decide	like	stop
consider	demand	love	try
defend	deserve	prefer	want
delay	fail	start	
deny	get (be allowed to)		
despise	happen		
discuss	hesitate		
dislike	hope		
enjoy	intend		
imagine	learn		
involve	manage		
keep	offer		
mention	plan		
mind	pretend		
miss	refuse		
postpone	seem		
put off	swear		
practice	tend		
recall	vow		
recollect	wait		
recommend	yearn		
report			
resent			
resist			
risk			
suggest			
tolerate			
understand			

Unit **13**
Participle Adjectives

Verb	Present Participle (-ing)	Past Participle (-ed)
alarm	alarming	alarmed
amaze	amazing	amazed
annoy	annoying	annoyed
astonish	astonishing	astonished
bore	boring	bored
challenge	challenging	challenged
charm	charming	charmed
comfort	comforting	comforted
compel	compelling	compelled
depress	depressing	depressed
devastate	devastating	devastated
disappoint	disappointing	disappointed
discourage	discouraging	discouraged
disgust	disgusting	disgusted
disturb	disturbing	disturbed
embarrass	embarrassing	embarrassed
entertain	entertaining	entertained
excite	exciting	excited
exhaust	exhausting	exhausted
horrify	horrifying	horrified
inspire	inspiring	inspired
intimidate	intimidating	intimidated
interest	interesting	interested
mystify	mystifying	mystified
please	pleasing	pleased
puzzle	puzzling	puzzled
satisfy	satisfying	satisfied
shock	shocking	shocked
surprise	surprising	surprised
tempt	tempting	tempted
terrify	terrifying	terrified
threaten	threatening	threatened
thrill	thrilling	thrilled
tire	tiring	tired
touch	touching	touched
worry	worrying	worried

Unit **22**
Responses to Suggestions

Acceptance

Okay.

Sure.

Cool.

Why not?

I can do that.

All right.

That's all right with me.

Fine.

That's fine.

That's fine with me.

Good idea.

That's a great idea.

Good thinking.

I like the way you think.

That's doable.

Hold on.

Hold on just a minute.

Wait a minute, please.

Wait a bit, and I'll do it.

That sounds like fun.

I'd love to help.

I'd love to do that.

Rejection

No, thanks.

Sorry.

Sorry, but no.

I'd like to, but I can't.

I wish I could, but I can't.

I don't have time now.

I don't have time for that now.

I'm not interested.

I'm not interested in that.

That's something I don't want to do.

I don't want anything to do with that.

You'd better ask someone else.

I can't do that, but maybe someone else can.

I'd love to help you, but I can't.

I'm busy now.

I'm too busy now.

That's not possible.

There's no way I can do that.

You'd better talk to someone else.

That's not going to happen.

I'd rather do something else.

I've got plans.

I've already got something planned then.

Common Exclamations

Yay!

Hooray!

Yeah!

Oops!

Oh, no!

Uh-oh!

Woah!

Eek!

Drat!

Darn!

Rats!

Yahoo!

Boo!

Wow!

Unit 28
Separable and Inseparable Verbs

Phrasal Verb	Separable or Inseparable	Meaning
ask out	separable	to ask someone to go out on a date
bring about, bring on	separable	to make something happen
call back	separable	to return someone's telephone call
call off	separable	to cancel
call on	inseparable	1) to ask someone to do something 2) to visit
call up	separable	to call someone on the telephone
catch up	inseparable	to become equal or to reach the same level
check in, check into	inseparable	to register at a hotel or travel counter
check out	inseparable	to leave a hotel
check out of	inseparable	to leave a hotel
cheer up	separable	to make someone happy
clean up	separable	to tidy or to make clean
come across	inseparable	to find
cross out	separable	to eliminate
cut out	separable	to remove something or to stop doing something annoying
do over	separable	to repeat
drop by	inseparable	to visit unexpectedly
drop in	inseparable	to visit unexpectedly
drop off	separable	to leave something somewhere
drop out	inseparable	to stop attending a class
figure out	separable	to understand
fill out	separable	to complete a form
fill in	separable	to complete spaces on a form
get along with	inseparable	to have a good relationship with
get back from	1) inseparable 2) separable	1) to return from somewhere 2) to receive something originally lent to another person
get in	inseparable	to enter
get off	inseparable	to leave a bus, train, or airplane
get on	inseparable	to enter a bus, train, or airplane
get out of	inseparable	to leave a car
get over	inseparable	to recover
get through	inseparable	to survive
get up	inseparable	to stand up
give back	separable	to return
give up	separable	to stop trying
go over	inseparable	to review
grow up	inseparable	to become an adult
hand in	separable	to give an assignment or project to a teacher

hang up	separable	to replace the telephone in the receiver
keep out	separable	not to enter
keep up with	inseparable	to stay at the same level
kick out	separable	to ask to leave
look after	inseparable	to take care of
look into	inseparable	to investigate
look out for	inseparable	to watch for
look over	separable	to review
look up	separable	to try to find information
make up	separable	to invent
pass away	inseparable	to die
pass out	1) inseparable 2) separable	1) to faint 2) to distribute
pick up	separable	to lift
pick out	separable	to choose
point out	separable	to identify
put away	separable	to put in the proper place
put off	separable	to delay
put on	separable	to get dressed or to dress someone
put out	separable	to extinguish
put up with	inseparable	to tolerate
run into	inseparable	to find or to meet
run across	inseparable	to find or to meet
run out of	inseparable	to come to the end of something
show up	inseparable	to appear
show off	separable	to demonstrate something of envy
shut off	separable	to stop something from running
take after	inseparable	to be like someone
take off	separable	to remove
take out	separable	1) to remove 2) to go on a date with someone
take over	separable	to take control
take up	inseparable	to begin
tear down	separable	to demolish or to destroy
tear up	separable	to rip into pieces
think over	separable	to consider or to ponder
throw away	separable	to discard
throw out	separable	to discard
throw up	inseparable	to vomit
try on	separable	to test
turn down	separable	to reduce
turn in	separable	to go to bed
turn off	separable	to stop a machine
turn on	separable	to start a machine
turn out	separable	to put out a light
turn up	separable	to increase

NOTE

NOTE